Rebecca Gilman

boy gets girl

Rebecca Gilman is the recipient of the Roger L. Stevens Award from the Kennedy Center Fund for New American Plays and a Jeff Award for new work, both for *Spinning into Butter*, which premiered at the Goodman Theatre and received its New York premiere at Lincoln Center Theater. Her play *The Glory of Living* premiered at the Circle Theatre in Forest Park, Illinois, and went on to receive a Jeff Citation, an *After Dark* Award, and the American Theatre Critics Association's Osborn Award. *The Glory of Living* was produced in London at the Royal Court and subsequently received the George Devine Award and the *Evening Standard* Award for Most Promising Playwright. Ms. Gilman is also the recipient of the Scott McPherson Award and an Illinois Arts Council playwriting fellowship.

A native of Alabama, Ms. Gilman now lives in Chicago.

boy gets girl

a play by
Rebecca Gilman

ff Faber and Faber, Inc.
An affiliate of Farrar, Straus and Giroux / New York

FABER AND FABER, INC.
An affiliate of Farrar, Straus and Giroux
19 Union Square West, New York 10003

Printed in the United States of America

Designed by Gretchen Achilles

FIRST EDITION, 2000

Second printing, 2000

Library of Congress Cataloging-in-Publication Data

Gilman, Rebecca Claire.
 Boy gets girl: a play / by Rebecca Gilman.—1st ed.
  p. cm.
 ISBN 0-571-19983-6 (alk. paper)
  1. Women journalists—Drama. 2. Stalking victims—Drama.
 3. New York (N.Y.)—Drama. I. Title.
 PS3557.I456 B6 2000
 812´.54—dc21   *99-089185*

to Charles

boy gets girl

Cast of Characters

The world premiere of *Boy Gets Girl* was presented by the Goodman Theatre in Chicago, Illinois, on March 13, 2000. It was directed by Michael Maggio. Sets were designed by Michael Philippi, costumes by Nan Cibula Jenkins, lights by John Culbert, and sound by Michael Bodeen and Rob Milburn. The dramaturg was Susan V. Booth and the production stage manager was Alden Vasquez. The cast was as follows:

THERESA BEDELL	*Mary Beth Fisher*
TONY	*Ian Lithgow*
HOWARD SIEGEL	*Matt DeCaro*
MERCER STEVENS	*David Adkins*
HARRIET	*Shayna Ferm*
MADELEINE BECK	*Ora Jones*
LES KENNKAT	*Howard Witt*

Characters

THERESA BEDELL, *thirty-five to forty*
TONY, *thirty to thirty-five*
HOWARD SIEGEL, *fifties*
MERCER STEVENS, *thirty-five*
HARRIET, *twenty-one*
MADELEINE BECK, *forty*
LES KENNKAT, *seventy-two*

Time and place

Various locales in New York City, in the present

act one

Scene one

A table in a bar, two chairs. TONY *sits alone, a little nervous, waiting for someone. He is an attractive man in his thirties. He is drinking a beer.* THERESA *enters, a bit hesitant. She carries a big bag, looks a little flustered. They stare at each other for a second.*

THERESA Tony?

TONY Theresa? *(They laugh awkwardly.)* Hi. *(He rises, offers his hand, she shakes it.)*

THERESA I'm sorry I'm late.

TONY It's okay.

THERESA No, I just . . . I didn't want you to be sitting here thinking I wasn't going to come. I mean, I wouldn't do that. I tried to call but I can't get my phone to work. They gave me this new phone . . . *(She pulls a cellular phone out of her bag.)* And I don't know. The display thing comes on but then I can't get a dial tone. *(She pushes a button, listens, holds it out to* TONY.*)* Do you know anything about these?

TONY No. *(Takes it, listens.)* I don't think it's working.

THERESA Anyway, I'm really sorry.

TONY It's okay, really.

THERESA Well, anyway. Hi.

TONY Hi. *(Beat.)* Do you want to sit down?

THERESA Yeah. I think, though, I might get a beer.

TONY Let me get you one.

THERESA No. It's okay.

TONY Let me get you one. What would you like?

THERESA Whatever. Just nothing dark.

TONY Do you want a Weiss beer?

THERESA Is that the big tall one?

TONY Yeah.

THERESA I don't think so. Just an, you know, an ale or some-thing. *(He starts off.)* Let me give you some money.

TONY No, you can get the next one. Okay?

THERESA Okay. *(He exits. She sits. The phone rings. She quickly answers it.)* What? . . . Oh, hey. Don't call me on the phone . . . *(She looks to where* TONY *exited.)* I lied, I said it was broken and I couldn't call. I was late. *(Beat.)* Well, I was thinking I wouldn't come. I was just sort of walking around. *(Beat.)* Look, I came, I'm here, so don't, you know, get all . . . whatever. *(Beat.)* He's fine, I guess. I've been here two minutes. *(Beat.)* I've been here two minutes and I don't know. All right? *(Beat.)* Okay, you know what? I'm hanging up now. *(Beat.)* I'll call you tonight. *(Beat.)* I'm pretty sure I'll be home in time to call you. *(Beat.)* No, he's fine. I'm not saying that. *(*TONY *enters with a beer, gives her a slightly puzzled look. She's been watching, knows he's coming. She makes a motion to him for one more second.)* I'm going now. Goodbye. *(Moving the phone away)* Goodbye. *(She looks for a button, hangs up. To* TONY*)* That was Linda.

TONY Really?

THERESA *(Looking at the phone)* I guess people can call in, but I can't call out.

TONY What did she want?

THERESA She wanted to know how it was going.

TONY You just got here.

THERESA That's what I told her.

TONY Oh. *(Small beat.)* I got you an India Pale Ale. Is that okay?

THERESA That's great, thanks. It used to be a lot easier when everybody just drank Miller High Life.

TONY I never had Miller High Life.

THERESA Well, if you had been living the high life you would have. *(Beat.) I mean,* it's the champagne of beers.

(Beat.)

TONY Maybe I should try it.

THERESA No. I'm sorry. You know, I have kind of a dumb sense of humor. I'm usually not serious when I say stupid things like that.

TONY Oh.

THERESA I mean, it's obviously not very funny either, so don't feel bad.

TONY No, I mean . . . I'm sorry, too. I guess I'm a little nervous.

THERESA Me, too.

TONY Really?

THERESA Yes.

TONY Oh, good. I mean, not good you're nervous, but good I'm not alone.

THERESA I understand.

TONY I've never actually been on a blind date before.

THERESA Really?

TONY Have you?

THERESA Tons. Nobody who actually knows me will go out with me. *(Beat.)* That was a joke.

TONY *(Laughs.)* Sorry.

THERESA I'll just stop trying. No, actually, I had a blind date in high school once, when I was a junior. I was supposed to meet this guy from another school at a party and when I did, he asked me if I wanted to go out to his van and "fool around" and I said I had to go to the bathroom and left with some friends. *(Beat.)* I guess I probably shouldn't tell you that, on your first blind date, how I just ditched some guy.

TONY I think it's good you ditched him. I mean, anybody with a van.

THERESA *(Smiles.)* Exactly. What'd you drive in high school?

TONY A Dodge Dart.

THERESA Cool. I drove a Chrysler Cordoba.

TONY With fine Corinthian leather.

THERESA Exactly.

(Small beat.)

TONY So you know Linda from work?

THERESA I do. Before she quit to go off and have babies and everything, she was my research assistant.

TONY You know, I have to make a confession: I've never read your magazine.

THERESA Well, first of all, it's not my magazine, and second of all, don't worry about it.

TONY What sort of stuff do you write?

THERESA All sorts, really.

TONY Do you get to pick? I mean, what you write about?

THERESA Usually. A couple of weeks ago I did a story about Edith Wharton's upstate estate. *(Small beat.)* That was kind of hard to say. Upstate estate.

TONY I don't . . . I don't know who she is.

THERESA Oh, she's a writer. She's dead, first of all. But she was a New York writer from the turn of the century.

TONY Is she really famous?

THERESA I guess her most famous book is *Age of Innocence?*

TONY Oh, with Winona Ryder?

THERESA Exactly. So, that was interesting. But then, I do get assignments still and it's usually something annoying. Like, on Thursday, I have to go interview Les Kennkat.

TONY The filmmaker?

THERESA I think "film" is a generous term.

TONY I thought he was dead.

THERESA So did I, actually. *(They laugh.)* So you met Linda through her sister?

TONY Right. I met Sarah at Michigan.

THERESA Right.

TONY And when I moved here, you know, I looked up everybody I even vaguely knew because I was terrified—this is the first big city I ever lived in—

THERESA Where are you from?

TONY Terre Haute?

THERESA The home of Eugene Debs.

TONY Yeah.

THERESA And Theodore Dreiser and Paul Dresser.

TONY I guess so.

THERESA On the banks of the Wabash.

TONY It is. Have you been there?

THERESA No.

TONY Oh. Well, anyway, I looked up Sarah, and then, my
   first Thanksgiving here, she took pity on me and took me
   along to Linda's for turkey. Then, I guess you know, Sarah
   moved to Boston last spring. But that's how I met Linda.
   But I have to be honest, I don't know Linda well. I mean, I
   hardly ever see her.

THERESA I don't know her well either and I see her all the
   time.

TONY Oh. Is she . . . I mean, do you not get along?

THERESA No, we get along fine. She just . . . she's certain she
   knows how I should live my life and she's always telling me
   what to do next.

TONY Like, maybe, go on a date with me.

THERESA Like, maybe that, but that's okay.

TONY Good.

(Beat.)

THERESA How long have you lived here?

TONY Four years.

THERESA Do you like it?

TONY I do now. I really hated it at first. I just thought everybody was so mean and it's so dirty here.

THERESA I know.

TONY But after a while it started to grow on me, and now, I
   mean, this might sound weird, but part of what I like about
   it now is how big it is. I like being able to just blend in.
   There are so many people, I just feel anonymous. I don't
   know what that says about me . . .

THERESA I agree. I think it makes you a little less self-involved.

TONY Right.

THERESA So what do you do?

TONY I do computer work. I work for KCS, and what they do is, they go into a business and design software specifically for the business, and then I go in and train people how to use it.

THERESA Do you like it?

TONY I like the work itself, but the thing I don't like is that I move around to a new site every two or three months, so I never really get to know anybody I'm working with. Or even if I do, it's sort of like, what's the point because I'm never going to see them again.

THERESA I see.

TONY *(Beat.)* But anyway, I don't want to ramble.

THERESA You're not rambling.

TONY I know we only agreed to have a beer tonight . . .

THERESA Yeah.

TONY So if you need to go, or whatever, I understand . . .

THERESA Oh. Do you want me to go?

TONY No, no. I was actually going to ask you before you went . . . I mean, not to be too forward or anything, but I thought I'd just go ahead and ask if you'd like to do something this weekend?

THERESA Just to get it on the table.

TONY Yeah, just to get it on the table.

THERESA Yeah. You know? I would like that.

TONY Great. We could have dinner maybe.

THERESA I can't do anything Friday night because I have to cover this benefit thing, but I'm free on Saturday.

TONY Saturday would be great. What's the benefit?

THERESA Some MoMA thing to get some MoMA thing going so MoMA people can give money to MoMA.

TONY You don't like MoMA?

THERESA Oh, sure, of course. I just don't like being around rich people. Have you ever noticed how rich people eat a lot when there's free food? Then poor people like me go hungry because we can't get to the buffet?

TONY You could stand to eat more, too.

THERESA Oh. Thank you, I guess.

TONY You're really thin.

(Pause.)

THERESA So what do you do when you're not working?

TONY Well, I run every day, and I like to do all the usual stuff, you know. Go to movies and read and watch TV and all that. Go for long walks. *(Small beat.)* That was a joke.

THERESA It was?

TONY Yeah. You know how, in the personals, everybody says they like to go for long walks. I always figured, if all those desperate single people really went for those long walks, eventually, wouldn't they run into each other?

THERESA Eventually, wouldn't they all find each other in the park?

TONY Yeah.

(They laugh.)

THERESA Do you like baseball?

TONY I'm not a big sports guy. I still follow Michigan football.

THERESA Don't they have the largest college stadium in the country?

TONY I don't know. Do you like baseball?

THERESA Oh yeah.

TONY Yankees or Mets?

THERESA Yankees, please.

TONY The only women I ever knew who liked sports liked them just because their boyfriends did.

THERESA Oh yeah?

TONY Did you have a boyfriend who was a big Yankees fan or something?

THERESA No.

(Pause.)

TONY My dad was a huge Cardinals fan.

THERESA Really?

TONY Yeah, well, any kind of sports, really, he was just a fanatic. Which is where, I guess, the word "fan" comes from, obviously. He was always pushing me to play football, when I was in high school, and I really didn't want to, but my mom talked me into it, because she said . . . well, her reasoning was that we didn't get along, my dad and me, because we didn't have much in common, so this way we would have some sort of connection. But I was really terrible at it, I'm sure in large part because I hated it so much, and so all it really did was give him another excuse to make fun of me. And then, you know, I just felt completely betrayed by my mother.

THERESA I'm sorry.

TONY Oh. Well . . . *(Suddenly very self-conscious. Making a* *joke of it)* "And that's why I'm so fucked up today."

(THERESA *laughs.*) I'm sorry, I didn't mean to get into all that.

THERESA I won't ever mention the Yankees around you again.

TONY No, no. Not that. Maybe you could take me to see a Yankees game sometime and I could learn to love them, too.

THERESA Maybe so.

TONY When does baseball season end?

THERESA At the end of September if they don't make the play-offs.

TONY Oh.

THERESA But they will.

TONY Well, maybe we could go see them now.

THERESA Well, first of all, they're out of town for a while, and second of all, let's not move that fast.

TONY Oh. I'm sorry.

THERESA It's okay, I just . . . you know.

TONY Right. *(Beat.)* So tell me, what's your favorite story? That you ever wrote?

THERESA Boy, that's a hard one. I don't really have a favorite.

TONY Did you study journalism in college?

THERESA I was a history major in college, but I wrote for the school paper, and then I went to graduate school in journalism at Indiana Bloomington.

TONY Oh! I think Linda mentioned that, but I forgot. So you were in Bloomington.

THERESA Yeah.

TONY What years?

THERESA It was . . . twelve . . . fifteen years ago.

TONY Then I was actually . . . I was just starting at Michigan then.

THERESA Oh, man, I'm older than you.

TONY You're robbing the cradle.

THERESA Yeah.

TONY I had a guy tell me once that men who go out with older women really want to have sex with their mothers. But I don't think that's true. Do you think that's true?

(Beat.)

THERESA I wouldn't know. But I think I'm only about three years older than you are, so . . . *(Beat.)* Was that . . . ? Was that a joke?

(Small beat.)

TONY *(Lying)* Yeah.

THERESA Good, because you scared me there for a second.

TONY See? I, too, have a dry sense of humor.

THERESA I do see. You might actually outdo me, dryness-wise.

TONY I think we have a lot in common.

THERESA Well, we'll find that out, won't we?

TONY We will. *(Pause.* THERESA *finishes her beer.)* Do you want another one?

THERESA Um, actually, I do have some work I need to do tonight. I've got a deadline tomorrow. And I was just . . . I was just planning on the one beer actually. So I think I'll go.

TONY But we're still on for Saturday?

THERESA Absolutely.

TONY Can I walk you home, or . . . ?

THERESA I think I'm just going to grab a cab.

TONY Where do you live?

THERESA Upper East Side. It's, you know, dull but quiet.

TONY Which street?

THERESA Um . . . Seventy-fourth.

TONY Near the park?

THERESA Near the park, yeah.

TONY I live down on Perry. Do you know where that is?

THERESA I do. Nice neighborhood.

TONY I like it. There are a lot of nice bars and restaurants. Little shops and stuff. There's one place down there called Allison's? (THERESA *shakes her head.*) It's just a little place but they have really good food and it's not too expensive. I go in there enough, they sort of know me there.

THERESA That's nice.

TONY Maybe we could go there Saturday night.

THERESA Sure. That'd be great.

TONY I'll call you, then, later this week, and we can set up a time.

THERESA Okay.

TONY Maybe Thursday or Friday, during the day. Can I call you at work? I mean, is that okay?

THERESA That's fine. If I'm not there, just leave me a voice mail message.

TONY I don't know if I have your home phone number.

THERESA If you don't get me at work, just leave a message and I'll call back.

TONY Okay. *(Beat.)* Well, it was very nice to meet you, Theresa.

THERESA It was very nice to meet you.

TONY I'd say Linda did good.

THERESA Yeah. *(He makes a move as if to kiss her; she holds out her hand.)* Thanks for the beer.

TONY *(Shaking her hand)* I'll see you Saturday.

Scene two

The following day; Theresa's office. A large bouquet of flowers is on her desk. Her boss, HOWARD, *is waiting for her, reading something.* THERESA *enters, carrying several pages of manuscript.*

THERESA Here you go. Thanks for waiting.

HOWARD Flowers came.

THERESA Look at that.

HOWARD Who are they from?

THERESA You.

HOWARD No.

(THERESA *takes the card and opens it, reads.)*

THERESA They're from this guy.

HOWARD Are you dating somebody?

THERESA No. I had one date with this guy last night. It wasn't even a date. It was a beer.

HOWARD He must have been really taken with you.

THERESA I guess he was. I don't know. I thought I was pretty unimpressive.

HOWARD What does the card say?

THERESA "It was really nice meeting you—Tony."

HOWARD Tony.

THERESA Yeah.

HOWARD Well, you should be very flattered. He obviously really liked you.

THERESA I guess so. *(Changing the subject)* So I read the new guy's story.

HOWARD Would you stop calling him that? He's been here three months.

THERESA Sorry. I read *Mercer*'s story, and I think it's good, for what's there, but I think it's only half a story.

HOWARD How's that?

THERESA *(Flipping pages)* Well, he ends with "the term 'literary friendship,' finally, seems an oxymoron, and so much of one that it borders on pretentious ludicrocity." Which . . . okay, first of all, "ludicrocity"? I looked it up and it is a word, but isn't it kind of a stupid word?

HOWARD Yeah.

THERESA And then, to be fair, he doesn't look at any literary friendships that were good. I mean, he only focuses on the ones in which people are betrayed or hurt.

HOWARD Are there any good ones?

THERESA Sure. I mean, go back just a little ways and start with William Dean Howells and Mark Twain, and Howells and Henry James.

HOWARD Who is William Dean Howells?

THERESA Oh, he's really great. His novels are great. *(Appraising him)* I can't believe you've never heard of William Dean Howells. You're an editor.

HOWARD I drank my way through college. Is there somebody else he can look at? Who's still alive?

(The phone rings.)

THERESA I'll let the voice mail get it.

HOWARD You can forward it straight to voice mail and then it doesn't even ring.

THERESA I know. It's just too much trouble.

HOWARD It's a button. You press a button.

(The phone stops abruptly.)

THERESA Okay. I think William Styron and Arthur Miller are friends.

HOWARD They're not going to talk to us.

THERESA Why not?

HOWARD They're just not. There's just an echelon that doesn't return our calls. They'll call *The New Yorker* back, but they won't call us.

THERESA You have such an inferiority complex.

HOWARD It's true, though. *(The phone rings again.)* Just answer it. *(Picking it up)*

THERESA Yeah? *(Beat.)* Oh, hi, Tony, how are you? *(Beat.)* Yes, I did get the flowers. They're very pretty. Thank you. I was going to call, but, um, I'm in a meeting. *(HOWARD gets up to go, she motions him back.)* I do like irises, too. Maybe they're out of season. *(Beat.)* Eight would be fine.

Why don't you give me the address now so I can meet you. *(Beat.)* No, you don't have to pick me up. *(Beat.)* No, Tony, it would be silly to have you come all the way uptown and then just turn around and go back again. I'll just meet you there. *(Beat.)* Look, I'm a big girl, I can take a cab. *(Beat. Writing something)* Okay then. Eight on Saturday. *(Beat.)* I had a good time, too. *(Beat. Interrupting)* Look, Tony, I don't want to be rude, but I'm still in that meeting. *(Beat.)* No, no, it's okay, just . . . um, I'll talk to you later, okay? *(Beat.)* You too. Bye. *(She hangs up.)*

HOWARD You should have let him pick you up.

THERESA Why?

HOWARD He was trying to be gallant. You should have let him be gallant.

THERESA That's like a hundred and fifty blocks worth of gallantry, round trip. That's ridiculous.

HOWARD He wouldn't have offered if he didn't want to do it.

THERESA I'm not even sure I want to go out with him.

HOWARD Why not?

THERESA I don't know.

HOWARD When's the last time you dated somebody?

THERESA It's been a while.

HOWARD What about that one guy? That Mark guy?

THERESA Mark Carter?

HOWARD He was a nice guy.

THERESA He got transferred. To Kuala Lumpur.

HOWARD Why didn't you go with him?

THERESA He didn't ask.

HOWARD Oh. I'm sorry.

THERESA I wouldn't have gone if he had. We weren't that serious. And I don't want to live in Kuala Lumpur.

HOWARD Right.

THERESA I bet a lot of Kuala Lumpurians don't want to live in Kuala Lumpur.

HOWARD You like saying "Kuala Lumpur," don't you?

THERESA Yeah.

HOWARD Anyway, I'm just saying that I think you're not used to the attention. That it makes you uncomfortable.

THERESA You know what? I don't want to talk about my love life.

HOWARD Okay. So you think Mercer should try to balance this ludicrocity?

THERESA Yes, I do.

HOWARD Okay, then . . . *(Referring to what she handed him)* . . . I'll read this after lunch. When do you talk to Les Kennkat?

THERESA Next week.

HOWARD Good deal.

THERESA *(Overlapping)* But can't you find somebody else—

HOWARD *(Interrupting)* Don't ask me again, I don't have anybody else to do it. *(Beat.)* Theresa. I honestly don't.

THERESA *(Beat.)* Look, Howard, it's just that, with certain stories you give me, I feel like I'm writing for *People* magazine and that's not why I went into journalism.

HOWARD You have to take the good with the bad—

THERESA *(Overlapping)* After twelve years?

HOWARD Look, if it was up to me we'd only publish stories about saints and we'd print them on a hundred-percent recycled paper and we'd only sell ads to people who paid union wages, but there's this little thing called the bottom line, and if I don't pay attention to it, then I'm out of a job—

THERESA Yeah, yeah . . .

HOWARD And so, I may add, are you. *(Pause.)* So how many words can you give me on Mr. Kennkat?

THERESA Five thousand?

HOWARD Make it fifteen.

THERESA Ten.

HOWARD *(Beat.)* It's a deal. *(Indicating pages)* I'll get this back to you by five.

(HOWARD *exits.* THERESA *stands, then looks at the flowers. She is not necessarily pleased.)*

Scene three

A restaurant. TONY *sits at a table alone. They have finished their meal. He takes a bottle of wine from the ice bucket, refills Theresa's glass, freshens his own.* THERESA *returns to the table.*

THERESA Sorry it took so long.

TONY Are you feeling all right?

THERESA I'm fine. *(Beat.)* They had the TV on in the bar when I walked by. The Yankees are winning.

TONY Oh yeah? Do they go to the World Series from here?

THERESA Well, they have to clinch the division first, then

they go to a five-game play-off series. Then a seven-game series for the pennant.

TONY You're going to have to teach me all this stuff. I don't know any of this stuff.

THERESA It's not hard, really. Just read the sports page.
(Beat.)

TONY The waitress brought the check while you were in the ladies' room, and she sort of knows me, and she said we make a great-looking couple.

THERESA Really.

TONY I told her that I only looked good because I was with you.

THERESA That was nice.

TONY Look, I was sitting here . . . I feel like I've been talking about myself all night. Why don't you tell me about your family.

THERESA There's not much to tell.

TONY Brothers? Sisters?

THERESA I have a brother.

TONY Older, younger?

THERESA He's older.

TONY Do you not want to talk about him?

THERESA No, he's just, um . . . he moves around a lot, so it's been hard to really keep in touch with him.

TONY What about your parents?

THERESA They're both dead, actually.

TONY I'm sorry.

THERESA Thank you.

TONY I don't know what I'd do if mine died. I mean, I com-
plain about them all the time, but I think I'd feel so alone or
something. Although, if my dad died tomorrow, sometimes
I think I wouldn't really care. You know? I mean, I know
that sounds harsh, but he treats my mom like shit. I mean,
my mom is a saint. When I was growing up, she did so
much for me that other kids' moms wouldn't even think of
doing. You should have seen the lunches she made me.
Everybody else would have peanut butter and jelly sand-
wiches, right? She'd make me homemade pasties. *(Beat.)*
Do you know what a pasty is? *(He pronounces pasty with
a short* a.*)*

THERESA They're little, like, meat pies, right?

TONY *(Disappointed she knows.)* Right. But she'd make me
these pasties, and every day she'd put something different
in it. One day chicken, the next day steak. They were great.
And homemade cookies or a big slice of cake. I mean, I
was the envy of that lunchroom. People were always trying
to trade lunches with me, but there was no way. You know?

THERESA Sounds like she really . . . spent a lot of time in the
kitchen.

TONY Do you cook?

THERESA No, I don't.

TONY Why not?

THERESA I've just never enjoyed it.

TONY I love to cook.

THERESA That's nice.

TONY I think one person in a couple should always know

how to cook. My mom taught me to cook. But I'm glad she did, because it seems like more and more women don't cook these days.

THERESA More and more women have other things to do these days.

(Beat.)

TONY So are you like a, feminist?

THERESA I'm like that, yeah.

TONY I am, too.

THERESA Good.

TONY I mean, there are women I work with who know so much more about programming than I ever will, and I think how they used to not even have the opportunity to get those jobs, you know? I think that's completely unfair.

THERESA It is.

TONY But what I don't like are those women who are really strident about it. I mean, this might be a generalization, and I know I shouldn't make it, but it seems to me that some feminists really hate men.

THERESA Well, I guess it's not technically a generalization to say "some" women hate men. I don't know. I don't know. I don't really want to talk about it.

TONY You don't?

THERESA I mean I just . . . I can't speak for other women.

TONY But you don't hate men.

THERESA No.

TONY Good. Have you ever been married?

THERESA No, I haven't. Look—

TONY I was engaged when I moved to New York. I mean, not
when I moved here, before I moved here. Which is why I
moved. I was engaged to this girl from college and we were
going to get married and I had a job in Detroit. But she
broke up with me. I mean, it was before the wedding and
everything, she didn't leave me standing at the altar. But
that's really why I took this job in New York. I just didn't
want to be hanging around where I would run into her all
the time and all that and it was sort of an impulsive deci-
sion, but I felt like I really wanted to get out of Michigan.

THERESA I see.

TONY It took me a long time, though, after that, to trust anybody again.

(Pause.)

THERESA Look, Tony, this is really, probably, the most awk-
ward moment for me to tell you this, but I'm going to go
home.

TONY Are you sick?

THERESA No, I just, I'm tired, and I think I'm going to go on
home.

TONY Well, let me . . . I'll pay the check and I'll take you.

THERESA *(Getting her purse)* No, I want to go home by myself. If that's all right. *(Getting out her wallet)* And I'm going to go Dutch on this with you.

TONY No, this is my treat. Are you sure you're feeling all
right?

THERESA *(Taking out a couple of bills)* I'm fine. I'm just
tired.

TONY Well, maybe . . . I was thinking, if tomorrow's a nice day, maybe we could take a walk up around your neighborhood. Since you live near the park.

THERESA Okay. Um, look. I have a confession to make. I've been sitting here listening to you talk and I think you're a very nice guy and funny and smart and very nice.

TONY I'm glad.

THERESA But I just, I sort of realized . . . I mean, I don't know if Linda told you this, but I don't really date a lot.

TONY She didn't mention it.

THERESA I haven't dated anybody in a while. And I, I realized, while I was sitting here, that I just can't. I mean, I haven't because of my work, because I spend so much time on my work that it didn't seem fair to anybody to get into a relationship with them and then make them take second place to my work. Do you see?

TONY I guess.

THERESA It just wasn't fair. And then I thought, when Linda mentioned you . . . I thought, maybe I've changed. Maybe I could date someone. But I've been sitting here this whole time worrying about an article I have to get in on Monday and I realized I haven't changed. I'm just not a good person to be in a relationship with. I'm too selfish or something. I'm just, I'm not good relationship material. You know?

TONY I don't think that's true.

THERESA Well, I do. And I do think you're great, but I just don't think there's any point in pursuing this as long as I feel this way.

TONY *(Beat.)* Okay.

THERESA I'm really sorry.

TONY No, it's okay, I understand. *(Picking up the check)* But at least let me buy dinner.

THERESA I can't. It's too much.

TONY Look, I'm just trying to walk away with a little of my pride here. At least let me pay for the meal.

(Pause.)

THERESA All right, then. Thank you.

TONY You know, last night I turned on the TV and I saw there wasn't a game on. I thought, if there was a game, I'd learn some of the names of the players and then I could impress you tonight. Because, you know, when we first met, I just thought that you must think I'm an idiot.

THERESA I didn't think that.

TONY Because I don't read books like you do. I mean, I took a lit class in college and all that, but I didn't know who you were talking about the other night. That woman.

THERESA Edith Wharton?

TONY Yeah, her. Is it because I didn't know who Edith Wharton was?

THERESA No. I would never in my whole life not like somebody for not knowing who Edith Wharton was. It's just me. It's entirely me.

TONY Well, if you leave now, maybe you can catch the end of the game.

THERESA That's not . . . Please don't think that way.

TONY Last night, I even, I called the museum. I called MoMA and asked about that benefit, because I thought, That's something I never do. I live in New York, I should go to the museum. I should learn about art. But they said it was a five-hundred-dollar-a-plate dinner. So . . . *(Beat.)* I was just . . . I think I was feeling really lonely.

THERESA I'm sorry. But I really . . . I have to go.

TONY No, I'm sorry. I shouldn't lay all this on you.

THERESA It's okay. *(Beat.)* Take care of yourself. Okay?

TONY It was really nice to meet you. You know? I mean it. I mean, even if things don't work out. It was nice to meet you.

THERESA You, too. I mean, for me to meet you. Bye, Tony.

*(*THERESA *exits.* TONY *sits alone.)*

Scene four

Theresa's office. MERCER *sits at Theresa's desk while her research assistant,* HARRIET, *takes notes.*

MERCER Call his agent and see if he'll do something over the phone.

HARRIET Okay.

MERCER And then . . . What are you doing for Theresa this week?

HARRIET Um . . . *(Flipping back in her notebook)* I'm supposed to find out something about Thomas Jefferson.

MERCER That's what she said?

HARRIET Yeah.

MERCER Don't be nervous, Harriet. I know it's hard to be new, I'm fairly new myself. But everybody here is nice, so just ask when you don't understand something.

HARRIET I don't don't understand anything. I just forgot what she said.

(THERESA *enters, carrying a book.*)

THERESA *(Handing it to* MERCER*)* I think this is it.

MERCER Thanks. Now Harriet needs some clarification on something.

THERESA Okay.

HARRIET Um, you wanted me to look up something about Thomas Jefferson?

THERESA Right. It was an article in *The New York Times* about a Library of Congress exhibition of his letters. If you go online and look up Jefferson in the *Times* archives—do you know how to do that?

HARRIET Yeah.

THERESA Then that should get you started. I'm sorry I can't be more specific.

HARRIET That's okay, that's . . . thanks, that helps a lot. *(She exits.)*

MERCER What do you want with Thomas Jefferson?

THERESA I was thinking of writing an article about conspiracy theories. Can I have my chair back?

MERCER *(Moving)* Oh yeah. Your phone kept ringing, so I forwarded it to voice mail.

THERESA Thanks.

MERCER So, I took your advice, and I think you were right. And unlike Howard, I think it's interesting to read about dead people.

THERESA Me, too.

MERCER But I do think William Dean Howells is a little obscure.

THERESA He's not obscure! He's so good . . . !

MERCER Okay, okay, just hear me out. I thought, what I'd do is start with the Transcendentalists.

THERESA Okay. Emerson and Thoreau.

MERCER And Hawthorne . . .

THERESA And William Dean Howells. Hawthorne and William Dean Howells!

MERCER Okay, let's just . . . let's stick to this right now.

THERESA Okay, the Alcotts. And then Bronson Alcott introduced Thoreau to Walt Whitman.

MERCER Really?

THERESA Yeah. And then Whitman met Oscar Wilde when Wilde toured the U.S. You know, you could start with one author and follow them through their literary friendships— do like a six degrees of separation thing all the way up to the present.

MERCER I actually just wanted, like, four more inches for the article I have now.

THERESA It was just a suggestion.

MERCER And it's a good idea, but it's not the article I'm writing.

THERESA *(Smiles.)* I'm sorry. I have a tendency to be . . . prescriptive, so just tell me to shut up.

MERCER It's okay. I do the same thing.

(HARRIET *enters with* TONY.)

HARRIET Theresa? Mr. Ross is here to see you.

TONY Hi.

(Beat.)

THERESA Hi. Did you . . . did you call to get up here?

HARRIET Your phone was forwarded to voice mail so I said
he could come up.

TONY I was just running some errands and I thought maybe
you'd like to have lunch.

MERCER Go on, I'm through. Thanks for all this.

*(*MERCER *exits,* taking HARRIET *with him. Beat.)*

TONY I know I should have called first, but I couldn't get
through, and I thought, if you had a minute, maybe we
could get a sandwich and talk.

THERESA I don't. I'm sorry.

TONY Maybe we could just talk for a minute. I'm not, you
know, trying to ask you out or anything, I just wanted to
apologize. I feel like I probably came on too strong or
something and I was thinking about what you said, about
how you didn't think it was fair to ask somebody to take
second place in your life, and I thought later, you know, it
must have seemed like I wanted you to marry me or something. Which is not true. I just want to get to know you. I
just want us to be friends. *(Small beat.)* So I thought I'd
just see if you wanted to have lunch and maybe we can be
friends.

THERESA No.

TONY Sorry?

THERESA No. I want to make this clear this time. I don't think
we have anything in common and I don't want to be
friends. I don't want to see you again.

TONY Oh. *(Beat.)* Is it . . .

THERESA What?

TONY Well, you said you hadn't dated anybody in a long time, and I was wondering, are you afraid of intimacy or something?

THERESA No.

TONY Because I know a lot of women who really throw themselves into their work, it's because they're afraid of intimacy. I mean, they're afraid of their own sexual desires or sexual powers.

THERESA That's not it. Now, if you don't mind, I need to get back to work.

TONY You sound really like you're mad at me or something.

THERESA I just don't think there's any point in discussing this.

TONY I'm just trying to help you figure it out.

THERESA There's nothing to figure out. And you don't know me.

TONY I guess I hit a nerve.

THERESA That's not it. Now, if you would leave, I have a lot of work to do.

TONY *(Wryly)* So you're not hiding behind your work?

THERESA No.

TONY Okay, okay. I get the point. I'm sorry that you're so closed off or whatever that you can't even make room for a new friend. Because I'm a good friend. You can ask anybody. And that's all I want, really. I mean, I'm not one of those guys who pretends to be a friend but is really just waiting for you to fall in love with me. Although I think

you would fall in love with me because I'm pretty charm-
ing. *(Laughs. Stops.)* But you don't, because you're too
repressed or something to even let anybody near you.

So, it was my last shot, but I get what you're saying.

THERESA Good. And don't come back here again.

TONY All right! Don't call security. *(Laughing)* All right. Have
a good life, Theresa.

*(*TONY *exits.* THERESA *stands for a moment, then goes to her
door, watches him leave, then calls.)*

THERESA Harriet?

*(*HARRIET *enters.)*

HARRIET Yes, ma'am.

THERESA I don't . . . don't call me ma'am.

HARRIET I'm sorry.

THERESA No, Harriet, don't ever let somebody up here to
see me without my permission. Okay? That's rule number
one.

HARRIET I'm sorry. He said he was a friend of yours.

THERESA You didn't know, I know, but for future reference,
don't ever let anyone up here without my explicit permission.

HARRIET Okay. *(Beat.)* He's cute. Who is he?

THERESA How old are you?

HARRIET Twenty-one.

THERESA Okay . . . *(As if she wants to tell her so much, but
doesn't have the time)* Cute isn't everything.

Les Kennkat's office, that night. He is a movie producer and director of low-budget, sixties sexploitation movies. A big couch is in his small office with a clutter of boxes, posters, etc. He is dressed in a suit from the seventies. THERESA *is positioning a small tape recorder.*

LES You're going to tape this?

THERESA With your permission.

LES Sure, fine. *(*THERESA *takes out a notepad and pencil.)* You're gonna write it down, too?

THERESA I've never been accused of misquoting anybody.

LES Okay, then, that's good.

THERESA All right, Mr. Kennkat, what are you working on now?

LES You're just jumping right in?

THERESA I'm just jumping right in.

LES Great. Right now I'm working on videos, mostly. I got that going, but I want to make another feature film as soon as I find the right actress.

THERESA What's the film about?

LES I won't know until I find the actress.

THERESA So that's where you start?

LES Oh yeah, I've always done that. Because you have to work with the actress's attributes.

THERESA And what attributes do you look for?

LES Big tits.

THERESA I see. Anything else?

LES A nice ass is always good.

THERESA Anything else?

LES What else do you have in mind?

THERESA I don't know. Acting ability?

LES No, I don't really care if she can act as long as she has gigantic breasts.

THERESA Okay. And where do you find your . . . actresses?

LES They flock to me.

THERESA They do?

LES Sure. You want to know why?

THERESA Sure.

LES Because. These women want to show off their breasts. They know they have colossal tits. It's no secret to them. So I just give them the opportunity to do that. And by that, I like to think I do them a service. And I do the guys who want to see these tremendous breasts a service, too, because I give them a good story and a good deal of expert camera work for really showing off these breasts in optimum conditions. What I do is, I'll shoot the breasts from down here, you know, low down with maybe a blue sky in the background. Maybe just a touch of treetops and a blue sky with clouds as a backdrop for these beautiful supple breasts. To me, there's nothing more breathtaking than a gorgeous pair of tits just sort of floating in the treetops.

THERESA *(Smiling.)* So . . . *Ga-Ga-Girls Galore* . . . ?

LES *Ga-Ga-Girls Galore* is one of the movies I'm most proud of. Are you laughing at me?

THERESA No.

LES *(Not angry)* I'm very serious about my work.

THERESA I know, I didn't mean to laugh.

LES Don't apologize. I can't help it if I make people smile.

THERESA Okay. You're sort of a cult figure now—

LES I don't understand that, what does that mean, "a cult figure"?

THERESA Just that it's hip to be into your movies now.

LES The people that read your magazine, they think I'm hip?

THERESA Yeah.

LES Well, that's good, I have no problem with that. I like being a hip daddy among the young generation. What is this magazine, anyway?

THERESA *The World.*

LES Never heard of it.

THERESA Really?

LES No, is it new?

THERESA No, it's been around about a hundred years.

LES What is it? A fashion magazine?

THERESA No, it's a magazine on culture and politics and art and . . . crap like that.

LES Really.

THERESA Originally it was called *Window to the World.* It was targeted to the new middle class in New York. But after World War One, they dropped the *Window* part and started drumming up subscriptions across the country, trying to broaden its appeal. *(Pulling a card from her pocket)* See? That's our logo. The world in a little window.

LES Can I keep this?

THERESA Sure.

LES Theresa Bedell. Is that you?

THERESA Yeah. *(Beat.)* If you don't know the magazine, why did you agree to the interview?

LES I need the publicity. I don't care where it comes from. So what do I fall under? Culture, art, or crap?

(Beat. THERESA *looks at him.)*

THERESA Culture.

LES That was very diplomatic.

THERESA Have you always made . . . films about breasts?

LES Well, I did have a contract with Paramount Pictures when I was a young man.

THERESA Really?

LES Yes, and they wanted me to make movies about little orphan boys who live in abandoned buildings and learn to be thugs and then meet priests who reform them. Horse hockey like that. It was completely uninspiring. So I quit. And then, for a long time, I couldn't get any work and that was not fun at all. But then I met this girl who had breasts that defied gravity and I thought, Here's what I've been waiting for. So I sold my car and rented a camera and went to work. We shot the whole movie in ten days. I called it *Succubus.* Do you know what a succubus is?

THERESA Yes.

LES Not many people do, I found out. But that's what I wanted to name the movie, because that's what it was about. She-devils who take on beautiful womanly forms and seduce men and then, when they're satisfied sexually, eat them.

THERESA Right.

LES And it was a hit. And then I made *Succubus Meets Incubus*. And that was a bigger hit. And pretty soon I didn't regret leaving Paramount Pictures, and I can proudly say that there is not anywhere in existence some crappy movie about an orphan and a priest with my name on it.

THERESA Congratulations.

LES Not many people can say that. That they're proud of what they do.

THERESA I guess you're right. I'm usually proud of what I do, but sometimes if I don't think my work's good, I see Ernie Pyle staring down on me, reprovingly.

LES Ernie Pyle?

THERESA The World War Two reporter?

LES Yeah, yeah, I know who he is.

THERESA My journalism school was named after him. They keep Ernie Pyle's typewriter in this special window on the side of the building, next to a big picture of him. Sort of like a shrine.

LES I'm sure it's real nice, but we're not talking about you, are we? Ask me another question.

THERESA Okay. Well, how do you feel about the way in which your movies encourage men to objectify women?

LES My movies don't do that.

THERESA They don't?

LES No, my movies celebrate women.

THERESA By fetishizing their breasts?

LES See, now you're not smiling anymore. Now you're turning on me.

THERESA No, I'm not.

LES Just because I didn't want to listen to your little story about Ernie Pyle.

THERESA It's hardly an outrageous question. I can't believe you've never been asked it before.

LES I've been asked it plenty before and I have a standard answer: my movies celebrate women.

THERESA Okay. How?

LES They celebrate their beauty, so men can enjoy their beauty. And, I might add, they teach women how to be beautiful. That's another service I do.

THERESA That's ridiculous.

LES No, it's not. Everyone wants to be attractive to the opposite sex. I help show them how to do it.

THERESA Then why don't you make movies about penises floating around in treetops?

LES Nobody wants to see that. That's not what women look at anyway. Women go for tight asses.

THERESA No, they don't.

LES What, are you gonna tell me a woman looks at a man's face first? That's just until she can look at his ass.

THERESA I don't think that's true.

LES What do you look for first?

THERESA A good personality—

LES Yeah, yeah, if the guy was short and bald and had holes where his ears should be and was fat and stinky, you're gonna tell me that you wouldn't care as long as he had a good personality?

THERESA I thought we were talking about you.

LES It's hard to be high and mighty when you're faced with a guy with no ears, isn't it?

THERESA No ears is different from an un-tight ass.

LES But what do you see first? The good personality? Or the tight ass? *(Beat. She thinks.)* This ain't calculus here, it's the simple rules of physical attraction.

THERESA You see the tight ass first if that's what you're looking for.

LES Fine. Stick to your story. Be the sainted Virgin Mary if that makes you feel better. But I bet, chances are, you've got a type. Because we've all got a type.

(Small beat.)

THERESA So how about the fact that your movies perpetuate a stereotype of women as sexual predators?

LES Forget it, I don't want to get into this. I hear this crap all the time and I'm sick of it. Let's wrap this up. I gotta go.

THERESA Okay. I need to ask you some background questions. It'll take about ten more minutes.

LES Nah. I gotta go. *(He hands her a folder.)* Here's a press packet. That should answer anything you got.

THERESA What's the hurry, exactly?

(Beat.)

LES The Yankees are on. They could clinch tonight.

THERESA Oh. It was on in the cab when I came up. They were up by a run.

LES Then what are we sitting here for, let's go watch the game. Can I buy you a drink?

THERESA I don't know.

LES It's not a date or anything. You're not my type, if you know what I mean. *(Beat.* THERESA *regards him.)* I mean, you know, I would never put you in one of my movies.

THERESA I understood you the first time. *(Turning off the recorder)* I'll watch the game by myself.

LES *(Getting his own things to leave)* Suit yourself. Just don't crucify me in that article. I mean, let me speak for myself. I can speak for myself.

THERESA You sure can.

LES Are you sure you won't have that drink?

THERESA I'm sure.

LES I won't ask a third time.

THERESA You just did.

LES What?

THERESA You just did. And I'll say it thrice: no, no, no.

Scene six

Theresa's office, a week later. She is on the phone.

THERESA Linda, I'm not blaming you. You told me up front that you didn't really know him. And I agreed to go out with him. *(Beat.)* I agree. It would be nice to meet somebody. It would be nice to be in a relationship. I would like that. Things are going well for me and I would like that. But not with him. *(HARRIET enters with a big bouquet of flowers.)* Oh God, more flowers?

HARRIET I know, aren't they beautiful? *(She exits.)*

THERESA *(On phone)* Yes, more flowers. Now will you please

call Sarah and ask her to call him and tell him that I'm serious and to leave me alone. *(Beat.)* What do you mean Sarah doesn't like him? Why did you fix me up with somebody Sarah doesn't like? *(Small beat.)* Okay, Linda, you know what, you're right: I am blaming you. How's that? I am blaming you. *(Long pause.* LINDA *is chastising her.)* Okay, I'm sorry. I'm not blaming you. I'm just irritated and I haven't gotten much sleep. *(Beat.)* I know. Go to your play group. I'll talk to you later. *(She hangs up, then takes the card from the flowers and reads it. Disgusted, she calls)* Harriet?

HARRIET *(Enters.)* Yes, ma'am?

THERESA I don't want to see any more flowers in my office. I want you to go down to the desk in the lobby and tell the guard not to sign for any more flowers. If any flowers make their way up to your desk, I want you to destroy them before I see them. Do you understand?

HARRIET I guess.

THERESA You guess?

HARRIET I don't know. If some guy was sending me flowers, I'd be flattered.

THERESA Do you understand my instructions or not?

HARRIET I understand.

THERESA Then just do as I say.

HARRIET Okay.

THERESA And if you copy an article from the paper for me, please check to see if it's continued on another page, because otherwise I only have the first page and that doesn't do me any good.

HARRIET Oh God, I'm sorry.

THERESA Just try and be careful.

HARRIET I will. I'm sorry. *(She starts to go.)*

THERESA And would you take these flowers with you and throw them in the trash?

HARRIET Okay.

*(*HARRIET *exits with the flowers.* THERESA *reads the card again, then rips it up and throws it away.* HOWARD *enters.)*

HOWARD Do you have that Les Kennkat thing?

THERESA Not yet.

HOWARD Why not?

THERESA I need to ask him some more questions. He gave me a press packet, but it's twenty years old. Literally.

HOWARD Well, make another appointment with him and finish it.

THERESA Fine.

(Beat.)

HOWARD *(Motions after* HARRIET, *smiling.)* So I notice you've been getting a lot of flowers lately. Is this thing with this guy getting serious?

THERESA No. This thing with this guy is over!

HOWARD Okay, okay.

THERESA *(Overlapping)* Jesus.

HOWARD Okay. What's the matter?

THERESA I don't know. *(Beat.)* Do you think I'm paranoid?

HOWARD No. Why?

THERESA Because I think Tony, the flower guy? I think he's following me.

HOWARD Why?

THERESA Because I wouldn't return any of his calls.

HOWARD But why . . . I mean, what evidence do you have that you're being followed?

THERESA My home phone number's unlisted, but he got it somehow. Maybe Linda gave it to him. She says she didn't, but maybe she gave it to her sister and her sister gave it to him. I don't know. But anyway, he got it somehow. And last night, I got home about nine o'clock and I walked in the door, and turned on the light, and right when I did the phone rang and it was him.

HOWARD What'd he say?

THERESA He wanted to know if I'd gotten all the flowers. I told him not to send me any more flowers, and to stop calling me. And he said okay, but then I got flowers today with a note apologizing for the flowers.

HOWARD He's a shmuck.

THERESA What?

HOWARD He's a shmuck. He doesn't know what he's supposed to do, obviously. With women. He's probably shy.

THERESA I don't think he's shy.

HOWARD Have you seen him following you?

THERESA No, but he asked me where I'd been and I lied and said I'd been at work and he said, "Oh really." All sarcastic, like he wanted me to know that he knew I was lying.

HOWARD Where had you been?

THERESA It doesn't matter.

HOWARD But you were lying.

THERESA I don't have to tell him anything.

HOWARD I'm not saying you do. I'm just saying, you're not the

greatest liar, so maybe he picked up on that and that's why
he was being sarcastic. Not because he was following you.

THERESA Maybe. But I still felt like I was being watched.

HOWARD Are you feeling guilty about something?

THERESA What would I feel guilty about?

HOWARD Well, did you sleep with him?

THERESA No! Howard. Jesus.

HOWARD I had to ask.

THERESA No, you didn't.

(Pause.)

HOWARD All right, I'm sorry. Here's what I think: I think the
guy can't take a hint, is all. I'd say, just pretend he's not
there and eventually he'll lose interest.

THERESA I haven't been hinting. I've been directly stating.

HOWARD Well, you know how guys are. It takes a while for
things to sink in. For example, I was positive that Claudia
and I were going to get back together, until she served me
with divorce papers. Probably this guy is the same. He just
doesn't want to accept that it's over.

THERESA Maybe so.

HOWARD I'm not helping, am I?

THERESA I just don't think the situations are the same.

(Beat.)

HOWARD I wish I knew what to tell you, but this isn't really
my area of expertise. I haven't had a date since the Carter
administration.

THERESA *(Small beat.)* Maybe you're right. Maybe I should
just ignore him.

　　　　　　　　　　　　　　　　　　　Rebecca Gilman

HOWARD Okay.

THERESA I'll get that Kennkat thing to you by the middle of next week.

HOWARD Can you make it Monday?

THERESA All right. (HOWARD *exits. She stares out the door after him for a moment, then calls*) Harriet! Throw the flowers in the trash. Don't leave them on your desk.

(HARRIET *enters.*)

HARRIET I just thought if you didn't want them . . . they're so pretty. You keep throwing them all away and they're so pretty. It seems like a waste. (*Beat.* THERESA *stares at her.* HARRIET *gets it.*) All right. (*She exits.*)

THERESA (*To herself*) It's not a difficult concept. You put them in the trash.

Scene seven

Theresa's apartment: a small apartment with a futon couch/bed, desk, and lots of bookshelves. It is late Saturday night. THERESA *is fully dressed, sitting up in bed, working on a laptop. The phone rings, but she makes no move to answer it. After a couple of rings her machine picks up. Theresa's voice comes on.*

THERESA'S VOICE You've reached my machine. Leave a message.

(*Tony's voice comes on.*)

TONY Hi, it's me again. It's past one and I'm just hoping you're
all right. It's too late for you to be out by yourself, I think. I
know you don't really want to talk to me or anything, but
I'm just worried about you. I'm wondering if you've gone
out of town or something. I haven't . . . I mean, you haven't
answered your phone all night. But like I said, I did what
you asked, and I stopped sending you flowers. But what I
wanted to tell you, that I forgot to tell you before, is that I
had this idea that I would keep sending you flowers until
irises were back in season, because I know how much you
like irises. And I know you can get the hothouse kind, but I
don't think that's the same, really. But then, what do I
know? They probably grow them in hothouses all year
round. That's probably something you would know. But
anyway, I know you've been working hard lately and I want
to do something for you, but you won't let me send you
flowers, so I was just thinking, maybe you'd let me cook
you dinner? Maybe tomorrow night? I mean, you haven't
even seen my place yet. So give me a call when you get in,
because I'll be up. Okay? . . . Okay. Bye.
(The machine clicks. THERESA, *who has stopped working in
the middle of it, starts again. Pause. The phone rings again.
Her voice comes on.)*
THERESA'S VOICE You've reached my machine. Leave a message.
TONY It's me again. I just . . . I left that message to call me
when you got in and then I just had a thought: maybe
you're not getting in. Maybe you're sleeping with somebody

else right now. And the thought of that just made me feel like I wanted to throw up. I just want to know. If you're seeing somebody else I just want to know. I don't want you to think you have to spare my feelings, because if you think that, then you must think I'm some pathetic jerk. Which would make me very angry, Theresa, because I don't need your pity. I'm not asking for your pity for one fucking second. I just think that you owe me the truth. (THERESA, *who has been staring at her computer through this, suddenly loses it and makes a grab for the phone.*) I think you owe me at least that much after everything you—

THERESA *(Snatching up the receiver)* Stop calling me! Don't send me things, don't try to see me. Don't ever speak to me again! *(She hangs up.)* Jesus Christ! *(Beat. The phone rings again. Furious, she tries to unplug it, can't get the plug out, then rips the cord from the wall. Silence. She goes back to the bed, sits down. She is shaking. She looks toward the window.)* I mean it. *(She looks toward the window again. Something dawns on her. She quickly reaches over and grabs her bag and searches through it. Her cellular phone starts to ring from inside the bag. She finds the phone and turns it off. She sits for a moment and thinks, then she quickly turns off the lights. In the dark she gets up, goes to the door, and checks it. It's locked. Then she gets a chair and pushes it up under the handle. Then she goes into the kitchen and comes back with a butcher knife. She puts the knife down by the bed, then gets in and starts working again by the light of her laptop.)*

Theresa's office, the following Monday. She is sitting, looking tired, staring into space. MERCER *enters with her article.*

MERCER Hey.

THERESA Hey.

MERCER Do you mind if I close the door?

THERESA No. Go ahead.

(MERCER *closes the door, sits.*)

MERCER Howard asked me to read your piece.

THERESA That's okay.

MERCER Well, what he really did was, he asked me to rewrite it. I think he didn't want to talk to you himself, because he didn't want to hurt your feelings.

THERESA Is it that bad?

MERCER It's, um . . . in places it just seems confused, and there are holes in the narrative. I don't know how we got from A to B.

THERESA I need to interview him again, but I don't want to, because he's obnoxious.

MERCER I thought he was kind of funny. *(Beat.)* I mean, in a totally offensive way.

THERESA He is kind of funny. *(Beat.)* You know, if you want to rewrite it, you won't hurt my feelings.

MERCER I don't really want to.

THERESA Then I'll do it. It's my stupid story. I'll do it.

(Pause.)

MERCER How do you remember all the things that you remember?

THERESA What do you mean?

MERCER I feel like you remember everything you read.

THERESA I keep notebooks.

MERCER Really?

THERESA Yeah. I write down the title of the book I'm reading at the top of the page, and then I write down what seemed most important to me about the book and what ideas I got from it. And then I number the pages and keep an index at the back of the notebook. So I can find what I want, if I go back. *(Beat.)* I guess I'm really anal.

MERCER No, I think that's really smart. *(He studies her.)* I guess I'm just wondering if there's something wrong. I know we're not close, or anything, but since I've been here, I've come to think of you as the person who holds up the standard around here. And I guess I was a little shocked to see that you let it slip.

THERESA You know a standard was actually a staff, that soldiers used to hold. They were called standard-bearers.

MERCER I know. That's why I . . . that's what I meant. *(Beat.)* Is there something wrong?

THERESA My voice mail was completely full this morning.

MERCER You're really busy.

THERESA No, it was full of messages from someone I didn't want to hear from. From over the weekend.

MERCER Who?

THERESA Can I . . . if I tell you something, do you promise not to tell anybody?

MERCER Of course.

THERESA Because I think Howard wants to understand, but I don't think he does, quite. And my friend Linda and I are not really getting along . . .

MERCER What's up?

THERESA Do you remember that guy that came into the office that day?

MERCER That kind of goofy-looking guy?

THERESA Yes.

MERCER Is he the flower guy?

THERESA Yes.

MERCER Is he bugging you?

THERESA He's stalking me. I think. I mean, I don't know what constitutes stalking legally, but if he's not, then he's coming awfully close. I know now he's following me. I mean, he called me all night, Saturday night, before I . . . Well, I ended up ripping the phone out of the wall.

MERCER Theresa.

THERESA Then I turned the light off because I had the feeling he was watching me somehow. And then the first message here was . . . you know there's that time and date stamp, on the messages . . .

MERCER Yeah.

THERESA The first message was after that, after two in the morning on Sunday, and he said, "I saw your light was off." So he was watching. I live on the second floor. You can't really see in, I don't think. But it's not that high up.

MERCER What did he say?

THERESA Well, I had been screening my calls all night and he had been calling and calling, and I finally picked up the phone and yelled at him, which I shouldn't have done. But then he knew I had been home, so he called here to tell me how angry he was, and every message just gets . . .

MERCER What?

THERESA Angrier and angrier. He keeps saying over and over that he wants to hurt me. That he wants me to suffer, like him. That he wants . . . he wants to hurt me.

MERCER Did you save them?

THERESA Yes.

MERCER Can I hear one?

THERESA *(Picks up the phone, punches in a code. Hands the receiver to* MERCER.*)* That's the first one. They go on. *(*MERCER *listens. The message ends and he punches a button for the next one. He listens a while longer, then he looks at* THERESA.*)* Do you think I should be scared?

MERCER How many of these are there?

THERESA Twenty.

MERCER I think you should call the police.

Scene nine

Theresa's office, later that day. MERCER *is there with* THERESA *and* MADELEINE BECK, *a plainclothes police officer.* BECK *is listening to the messages while* THERESA *and* MERCER *wait.*

BECK *(Holding the receiver out)* That's the last one. How do I get out of here? *(THERESA takes the phone, punches buttons, hangs up. Overlapping)* Don't erase those. Do you have any other messages or letters or anything?

THERESA There are messages on my machine at home. And he sent me some e-mails, but I deleted them all.

BECK That's okay. Did you keep any of the cards he sent you?

THERESA No.

BECK If he sends you anything else, keep it. And from now on keep a diary of any time he calls, any time you see him. Any contact at all. Write it down, and write down the date and time. The more specific the better.

THERESA What am I doing this for?

BECK Well, I think with these messages, we can get you a temporary restraining order. But just in case. For future reference, you should keep the diary.

THERESA For future reference?

BECK Well, we can get the restraining order, but I'll tell you up front, it's hard to enforce it. If he doesn't want to be seen, he won't be. I ran a check on him when you called, and he doesn't have any priors, so if all he does is call you again, then we couldn't hold him for that. But if he builds up a record of consistent abuse, then we could definitely charge him.

THERESA Consistent abuse?

BECK Abuse of the restraining order. Not of you, necessarily.

THERESA Great.

BECK In the meantime, you can take some precautions. Get an unlisted phone number.

THERESA I had one, he got it.

BECK Get a new one, and don't give it to anybody except your closest circle. And since he knows where you live, you should go ahead and move.

THERESA Move?

BECK Do you have a doorman?

THERESA No.

BECK Well, when you move, move to a building with a doorman and get an alarm for your apartment. Also, before you move, I'd go ahead and change your name. Then put the apartment and the phone and everything in your new name.

THERESA Okay. I don't want to change my name.

BECK I know it's a hassle.

THERESA I'm a writer. I write under this name.

BECK You'll have to decide that one yourself. Okay, what else. Okay, make sure you vary your route to work and back. Never take the same route two days in a row, but don't fall into a pattern either. And vary your routine as well. If you go to the health club after work, start going before work or during lunch. If you go to church on Sundays, think about changing churches. Some people feel safer buying a gun, but I can't in good conscience recommend that. I've seen too many people shot with their own guns.

(Pause.)

MERCER Can I clarify something?

BECK Sure.

MERCER Are you telling Theresa to do all these things now? Or are you telling her this just in case she needs to know somewhere down the line.

BECK I think she should seriously consider doing them now. *(Beat. To* THERESA*)* I don't know. This escalated quickly, and I'll be honest, that concerns me. Most of the time, if somebody's being stalked, it's by somebody they had a substantial relationship with. Or a coworker or somebody who sees them every day and has been harboring a secret obsession.

(Beat. Both BECK *and* THERESA *instinctively look at* MERCER.*)*

MERCER Hey.

BECK No. I mean somebody like you, not you. So the rapidity of this concerns me.

THERESA I guess I should have called you sooner.

BECK Well, you could have called, but honestly, I couldn't have done anything, because he didn't threaten you until now. *(Beat.)* Don't beat yourself up, okay? I tell all my complainants that. You don't know. You think you can handle him yourself and then all of a sudden he's whacked out on you.

THERESA I guess I did think I could handle it myself.

BECK Unfortunately though, the very things you did to try and stop him from bothering you were probably the very things that egged him on.

THERESA How's that?

BECK Well, like if you pick up the phone and say, "Don't ever call me again," you think you're being clear, but all he's hearing is "She's talking to me. I still have a chance." And I don't know how you broke up with him—

THERESA I didn't break up with him. You have to have a relationship before you can break up, and there was none.

BECK Right. I just meant, I don't know how you left it. If you gave any kind of excuse, or left it open in any way, then he didn't hear you saying "No." He heard you saying "Yes, once this one thing changes, then we can be together." Like if you said you were still hung up on some other guy, or you weren't ready for a relationship. Any of those things you say.

THERESA I said it was my work.

BECK See? What you should have said was "I thought it over and I don't want to see you again," and not given a reason even if he asked.

THERESA This isn't doing me much good right now.

BECK No, I'm just saying . . . for future reference.

THERESA I don't need it, because I'm never going out with anybody again.

BECK That's up to you, of course. *(Beat.)* Okay. I can't think of anything else right now. The restraining order may very well scare him off. But you should be prepared for the opposite reaction, too.

THERESA Which is what?

BECK Well, that it pisses him off and he comes back at you even harder. That happens and it's another reason to take precautions.

THERESA What if none of this works, then what?

BECK You mean . . . ?

THERESA I mean, what's the worst that can happen?

BECK There's no reason to think about that.

THERESA Why not?

BECK There's just no reason to think about it.

THERESA Well, what's the worst thing you've ever seen?

BECK You don't want to know.

THERESA Have you seen people killed?

BECK I've seen that.

THERESA That wasn't the worst thing? *(Beat.)* Detective? *(Pause.)*

BECK You don't want to know.

act two

THERESA *is back at Les Kennkat's office, interviewing him.*

THERESA I appreciate your seeing me again.

LES Well, you said you wanted to get it right, and I want you to get it right, too.

THERESA So, I have some questions here. Just biographical stuff. You were in the war?

LES I was with a film unit. I was stationed in London. But that's all in the press packet. Ask me something else.

THERESA Okay. *(Scanning down a list of questions, obviously skipping several.)* Your marriage to Joy Box . . . I assume that wasn't her real name?

LES No.

THERESA . . . it ended after a year. What happened?

LES Her name was Kathy Malone. And she didn't like it that I slept around with other women.

THERESA Oh.

LES I was very fond of Kathy, but I couldn't change my spots, it turned out. She told me she would leave me, but I didn't believe her. But she did. She stuck to her guns, and I've always respected her for that.

THERESA Why didn't you believe her?

LES I don't know. I just didn't.

THERESA But if she said it . . .?

LES I don't know.

THERESA Why don't men take women seriously? Why is that?

LES I take women very seriously.

THERESA No. When a woman talks, a man just sees her mouth moving. I could say, "The ceiling's caving in" or "You stepped in gum"—something I could prove, empirically— and you wouldn't believe me.

LES I would believe you. Is the ceiling caving in? *(He looks up.)*

THERESA I didn't mean you. I meant, one. One wouldn't believe me.

LES The reason I didn't believe Kathy is simple. I didn't want to believe her. Okay? I wish I had. Then I wouldn't be sitting here—seventy plus—all alone. I'd have somebody to take care of me. I have health problems. I have problems with my colon and they might have to take it out. An old man without a colon doesn't attract women to him anymore.

THERESA Well, what do you expect?

(Beat.)

LES You know, I have been interviewed many times, especially in the old days. And even cub reporters from *Movie News* did a better job than you do. These have been two of the worst interviews of my life. After the last one, I went and got drunk. I couldn't believe how rudely you rejected me and my friendly offer of a drink. And now I want to go get drunk again. You're really a depressing person.

THERESA Well, so are you.

LES See, I don't think that's your job. To come in here and tell me I'm depressing. *(Beat.)* How am I depressing?

THERESA You're whining because the very women you treated like shit aren't here to take care of you in your old age.

LES I could always hire a nurse. There's nothing I like better than a voluminous pair of breasts in a tight white uniform.

THERESA Forget it.

LES I was just joking! You're so depressing you kill a joke before it even hits the air.

THERESA I could laugh at that, I guess. But I don't want to encourage you. And it's not funny.

LES Last time you thought I was funny.

THERESA Sometimes you are, I guess. Parts of your movies are funny. Not the breast parts, but the parts where people run over each other with cars and their arms fly off.

LES The comic relief.

THERESA Right. So I could say about you, "He's a funny guy, except when it comes to women." And I have said that before, about other men. You know: "He's a good guy, but he does have a problem with women." But I'm not saying that anymore. Because you're not a funny guy, and you're not a good guy, if you can't deal with half the population of the world. Your problem with women is a problem with more than fifty percent of the people on this planet, and that's too high a percentage to make you funny.

LES *(Nods, beat.)* I see what you're saying. If something offends you, then you're not going to find it funny. No matter what.

THERESA But do you see what else I'm saying? About how you can't deal with half the population of the world?

LES Sure, but neither can you.

THERESA That's not true.

LES No, you obviously can't deal with me.

THERESA But that's just because you can't deal with me. If you could deal with me, then I could deal with you.

LES Aw, forget it. This is stupid. Don't publish anything about me in your stupid magazine. I don't want you writing anything about me.

THERESA Well, you can't stop me.

LES Fine, go ahead. But believe me, you can't say anything worse about me than what I've already said about myself. Trust me. There's nothing in me that's surprising. People hear me talk about my passion for breasts and they think, What a sad old man. And they're right. I am a sad old man.

THERESA You're not going to make me feel sorry for you.

LES Obviously. You're heartless.

THERESA I'm not heartless.

LES Then stop tormenting me. I thought you were a reporter. I thought your job was to come here and ask me questions, which I then answer. Not to sit in judgment of me. But that's all you've done. All you've done is yell at me.

(Pause.)

THERESA Then I apologize for my lack of professionalism.

LES Apology accepted. You'll find I'm also a very forgiving man. Let's just put this behind us. Okay?

THERESA Okay. I just have a few more questions.

LES Shoot.

THERESA Your new project, do you have any actresses in mind for that?

LES I do. I just found a lovely young lady, Deena Delite, but I'm going to ask her to change her name because Deena Delite sounds cheap to me.

THERESA Do you have another name in mind?

LES Not yet, but something will come to me. Something always does. I usually come up with a good screen name for a woman by staring at her naked breasts.

THERESA I see.

LES Or fucking her. But I can't always do that anymore because old age has finally caught up with me in the nether regions. But even if I can't penetrate a woman, I can still bring her to orgasm with my tongue or finger.

THERESA *(Fairly jumping up)* Okay. That's all I need.

LES No, because what I'm saying is, that in that moment of ecstasy, when she's wet and moaning, that's when a name will come to me.

THERESA *(Putting her recorder away)* That's it! That's all. I don't need to hear any more.

LES When will this come out?

THERESA Next month.

LES *(As THERESA leaves)* And what's the name of the magazine again?

THERESA *(Already off)* The World.

LES *(Alone.)* That's right. Window to the world. The little world in a window.

Scene two

Theresa's office, a couple of days later. MERCER *is waiting for her.* HOWARD *enters with an article.*

HOWARD Did you read this?

MERCER Yeah.

HOWARD I can't run this.

MERCER I thought it was funny.

HOWARD She never lets up. Every reference. *(Reads from different sentences.)* " 'I always start with the actress,' says Kennkat, the seventy-two-year-old connoisseur of women's breasts." "For the past fourteen years, Kennkat, a die-hard fan of mammary glands . . ." "A breast buff from way back, Kennkat began his film career . . ." *(Trails off, smiles.)* It is sort of funny.

MERCER Run it. What's he going to do? Sue you for defamation of character? It's all true.

HOWARD Maybe I will. *(Beat.)* Where's Theresa?

MERCER I don't know, I'm waiting for her. We were supposed to meet at ten.

HOWARD *(Looks at his watch.)* Should we be worried?

MERCER I don't know. She hasn't heard from him in two weeks. I think the police might have been right. I think the restraining order scared him off.

HOWARD I hope so. The shmuck.

MERCER Yeah.

HOWARD I thought at first he was just smitten. But I guess what used to pass as smitten, these days, is psychotic.

Rebecca Gilman

MERCER Yeah. I guess.

HOWARD Or maybe that's going too far.

MERCER No, I think I agree.

HOWARD Well, I'm not sure I do.

MERCER I am. I've been thinking about it since this happened. You know, I was wondering, did I ever do anything to scare a woman before? Not intentionally, but did I ever do anything that came off as scary? And I know, when I was in college, I had a girlfriend who dumped me for another guy and I would call her dorm room, just to see if she was there, or walk out of my way to see if her light was on. But just a couple of times, you know. I didn't make a career of it.

HOWARD Everybody's done something like that.

MERCER I know. I think that's my point. It's not exactly abnormal behavior. But it's on the same continuum.

HOWARD I don't get you.

MERCER Normal, male, heterosexual behavior is somewhat psychotic. I was going to talk to Theresa about this first, but . . . I want to write about this. Can I write about this?

HOWARD Write about what?

MERCER Tony. Or guys like him. Because, when you look at Tony, he looks like a normal guy. And in a lot of ways, he is a normal guy. Or at least he's doing what normal guys do in movies. It's a classic romantic plot. First the guy sees the girl. He thinks she's beautiful; she has long brown hair and big brown eyes, she's just the sort of woman he's dreamed about, so bang—he falls in love with her. Regardless of the fact that he doesn't know anything about her, he falls madly, deeply in love with her. But there's some obstacle to his love. Like the woman's dating some jerk who's completely wrong for her. So our guy has to prove himself to her. And to do that, he starts following her around. He spies on her, and as he watches her, he becomes convinced that if they could only be together, she would love him. So he gets aggressive. He bombards her with flowers and rents a billboard to declare his love, then bursts in on her wedding and tells her she's making a terrible mistake. And she comes around. She dumps the jerk and at the end of the story she's kissing the guy. Even though the guy has basically been stalking her, his perseverance pays off. He gets the girl. So this Tony guy is probably wondering, Why don't I get the girl? A lot of guys are out there wondering, Why don't I get the girl?

HOWARD And what are the girls thinking?

MERCER They're thinking . . . I look great. Everybody's watching me. *(Beat.)* But I can't write that.

HOWARD Why not?

MERCER I'm a man. I can't write that.

HOWARD But it's true, isn't it? I mean, don't some women walk around thinking they look good?

MERCER I think some women do. I mean, sometimes I see a woman, and I think . . . whatever I think, and I think she wants me to look at her and think that. But I also think that's because she's been told all her life that she should want people to look at her. Just like I've been told that I'm the one who's supposed to do the looking.

HOWARD But how can you not look at people?

MERCER Well, it's not just looking at people. It's looking at people in a certain way. Like I'm checking out her ass.

HOWARD That's what I meant. How can you not check people out? It's what you instinctively do.

MERCER But do you look at a woman and think, There's an attractive woman. Or do you think, Nice ass.

HOWARD What's the difference?

MERCER I think the difference is in the intent. Maybe "There's an attractive woman" would lead you to try and get to know the person. "Nice ass" would be it. You'd stop there, you wouldn't care about the woman, you'd only care about her ass.

HOWARD But I've thought "nice ass" and then later I've gotten to know the woman. Then I know her, I like her, and she has a nice ass.

(Beat.)

MERCER Okay, maybe you would get to know her, but guys like Tony wouldn't. He would just assume that he knows her because he likes her ass. And what I'm saying is that you and me and Tony and all the other guys in the world, we all start in the same place. We all have the same training. We're taught to look at asses. And women are taught that they want to have their asses looked at.

HOWARD Who taught us that?

MERCER Everybody. Every ad on TV. Every song on the radio. Every *Esquire*. Every *Cosmopolitan*. Every Les Kennkat movie. Everybody.

HOWARD Les Kennkat doesn't really show asses, though. His movies are mostly breasts.

MERCER Asses or breasts, it's really academic.

HOWARD Okay. So Les Kennkat tells me to look at breasts.

MERCER Yes.

HOWARD Or does Les Kennkat know that I'm already looking at breasts, and he just takes advantage of that? I mean, men like breasts, right? It's a biological thing.

MERCER No, you think it's biological because you've been trained to think that, but it's really cultural. Different cultures like different things. I mean, do you like tiny feet?

HOWARD I like a nice foot.

MERCER But do you like teeny tiny feet?

HOWARD I guess not.

MERCER See, men in China used to like teeny tiny feet, so women bound their feet. Some tribes in Africa liked very long necks so the women put those rings around their necks, to stretch them out. At the turn of the century, apparently, men liked really huge butts so women wore these giant bustles to make their butts look huge. The size of breasts, even, goes up and down. Literally. You can get these breast implants now that you can inflate or deflate, according to the fashion.

HOWARD Where'd you see that?

MERCER The Internet.

HOWARD Huh. *(Beat.)* So you don't like large breasts?

MERCER Not particularly, no.

HOWARD You like small breasts.

(Beat.)

MERCER The point is, Howard, when I meet a woman with breasts I like—

HOWARD Small ones.

MERCER Whatever. Just because I like her breasts, it does not mean that I love her. And it does not mean that I know her. And if I stop at the breasts, I will never know her.

HOWARD Unless you know her in the Biblical sense.

MERCER Oh, for God's sake!

HOWARD I'm just kidding. It's a joke. Relax. *(Beat.)* So what is your article about?

MERCER It's about Tony and Theresa. And why the boy thinks he should get the girl, and why the girl thinks she's something to get got.

HOWARD *(Thinks.)* I think I see where you're going. I'm not sure I agree a hundred percent, but it's interesting.

MERCER So I can write it?

HOWARD Give it a try. We'll see how it goes.

MERCER Great. Thanks.

(Harriet enters with some letters.)

HARRIET Theresa's mail. *(She puts it on Theresa's desk.* HOWARD *and* MERCER *instinctively look at her breasts. She notices and looks down at her shirt.)* What?

HOWARD AND MERCER Nothing.

(Harriet exits.)

HOWARD *(Watching her leave)* How's she working out?

MERCER She makes a lot of mistakes and she talks on the phone all the time. But other than that.

*(*THERESA *enters.)*

THERESA Hey.

HOWARD Hey, you're late. You're supposed to call me so I don't worry.

THERESA I got rid of my cell phone. It made me feel too accessible.

HOWARD Well, get another one so you can call. What if there's an emergency?

THERESA All right. I was looking at apartments. I think I found a place.

HOWARD Is it secure? Is there a doorman?

THERESA Yeah, a doorman, and security cameras. The whole bit. I can't afford it. But I liked it and I really . . . I don't feel comfortable in my place anymore.

HOWARD How much more is it a month?

THERESA Four hundred.

HOWARD We'll work something out.

THERESA Are you giving me a raise?

HOWARD We'll work something out, okay? You take the place, though. Call them now so you don't lose it.

THERESA Okay, Howard. Thank you. *(She pulls a card from her purse and goes to the phone.)*

HOWARD And I read this Kennkat thing and I get the point.

THERESA He likes breasts?

HOWARD No. I get the point that you are not inclined to write these sorts of pieces anymore. *(Beat.)* You don't have to.

THERESA What?

HOWARD I've taken advantage of your loyalty and your reliability for too long, and you and I are going to sit down and decide on a new direction for the both of us, that pleases the both of us.

THERESA I want to write about the Yankees. The Yankees are the only thing good in my life right now.

(Beat.)

HOWARD Then you write about the Yankees.

THERESA Okay.

HOWARD Now get that apartment. *(He exits, quickly.)*

THERESA What got into him?

MERCER Guilt. Can I close the door?

THERESA Sure. You know, I think I'll get stalked every day. I get a raise, I get to write about the Yankees. *(Dialing the phone.)* I'm just going to call this realtor and then we'll talk about your story.

MERCER I'm in no hurry.

THERESA *(On the phone)* Hi. I was calling for Casey Samples . . . Sure, I'll hold. *(She starts flipping through her mail. To* MERCER*)* So what's your idea?

MERCER I'll wait till you get off the phone.

THERESA *(Still flipping through mail. As she talks, she opens something, glances at it, throws it away. Still to* MERCER*)* I haven't really left my house, you know, I've basically been going home and hunkering down. So I've been watching a lot of TV, and there's that cable channel, Lifetime? It's the women's network? *(Looking at a letter without opening it)* They play all these made-for-TV movies on there and, I don't know, every other night, I guess, there's one on about stalking. They're all called, like *Poisoned Love* or *Love Hurts*.

MERCER Or . . . *The Graduate.*

THERESA *(Laughs.)* Exactly. Anyway, they all start with a married woman, and her husband's ignoring her. But the tennis pro at her country club thinks she's really hot and he makes a pass at her. And she gives in and has sex with him, but she doesn't want to have a real relationship with the guy because he's a tennis pro, for god sake. But he won't have that and he starts stalking her. Then her husband finds out and leaves her. So she buys a gun to protect herself, and at the last minute, she shoots the stalker in the head. Sometimes it's a pistol, sometimes it's a pump-action rifle. *(Noticing a letter, opening it)* At first I was disgusted, but I found I kept watching the stupid things, because, at the end, I felt this real sense of satisfaction when the stalker got it in the head. *(Pause. She's reading the letter. It is very disturbing. Quietly)* Mercer? *(Someone comes on the line. On the phone. Urgent.)* Yeah, I want to get that apartment on Sixty-eighth. This is Theresa Bedell. *(Beat. Suddenly screaming)* What do you mean?! I was there twenty minutes ago! What do you mean?!

MERCER Theresa?

THERESA *(On phone)* Then you have to get me another one!

MERCER *(Overlapping)* Theresa? *(He goes to* THERESA. *As he rounds the desk, he sees the letter she was looking at, looks at it.)*

THERESA No! I don't . . . I can't wait! NO NO! Now! Do you hear me? NOW! You can't—we had a verbal contract! A verbal contract!

MERCER Oh God. *(Quickly turning over the letter)* Hang up the phone. *(He tries to take the receiver from her.)*

THERESA No!

MERCER Hang up the . . . *(He pulls it from* THERESA, *sets it down.)* Hang up the phone. *(She is shaking. He puts his arm around her.)* We'll call the police. It's just a letter. He's not here, he's not here. It's just a letter. *(Pause. He holds* THERESA, *then she gently pushes him away. He steps back.)* Okay.

THERESA *(Quietly)* I don't know you.

MERCER Okay.

THERESA What's your interest in me?

MERCER I'm just trying to help. Honestly. I promise I'm just trying to help. *(*THERESA *doesn't answer.)* Is there someone . . . why don't you let me call your friend Linda.

THERESA This is Linda's fault.

MERCER Is there somebody else I can call? Somebody in your family?

THERESA No.

MERCER Okay. I'm going to call the police, then. What's the woman's name?

THERESA Detective Beck.

MERCER Is it in your Rolodex?

THERESA Yes. Under "B." For Beck. *(She backs away from the desk as* MERCER *gets the number, dials. Talking to herself)* The play-offs are on tonight.

MERCER *(On the phone)* Can I speak to Detective Beck, please? . . . Thanks. *(Beat.)* Yeah. It's Mercer Stevens calling, it's about Theresa Bedell, it's urgent.

THERESA If he is watching the Yankees . . . if he is somewhere, watching the Yankees, I'll kill him.

MERCER *(To* THERESA*)* It's okay. They're paging her.

THERESA I mean it.

MERCER I know.

THERESA If the Yankees blow the play-offs, I'll kill them.
(Beat.)

MERCER Look, don't let me freak you out, okay? But if you want to come over to our place tonight, we've got a pull-out couch, and according to other guests, it's very comfortable.

THERESA We?

MERCER Me and my wife.

THERESA You're married?

MERCER Yes.

THERESA I didn't know you were married. You don't wear a ring.

MERCER I have a contact dermatitis. With metal.

THERESA You get a rash.

MERCER I get a rash. Right. *(Beat. Into phone)* Yeah, I'll keep holding. Thanks. *(Back to* THERESA*)* You know, I told Michelle the other day, though, that we should have you over for dinner or something. But I didn't know how to broach it. I'm not good at that stuff. I don't know how to make friends as an adult.

THERESA I see. I mean, I understand.

MERCER In college you'd meet somebody, and if you both really liked Aerosmith, you were best friends.

THERESA Right.

MERCER And I was thinking, maybe that's what happened with Tony. Maybe you said something, on that first date, that made him think you were perfect for each other. It could have been anything, really, because he already had a

picture of the ideal woman in his head, and he was just
looking for somebody to impose that on. You probably said
one little thing that fit the picture. Or you wore your hair a
certain way. Or he liked the shape of your *(Theresa is staring at him.)* he liked the way you looked.

(Pause.)

THERESA Is this it?

MERCER What?

THERESA Is this the idea? For the story? You want to write
about me and what's happening to me?

MERCER *(Hesitates for a moment, decides not to lie.)* It is. I
didn't mean . . . I mean this isn't the time to talk about it.

THERESA No. Go ahead. Tell me.

MERCER Maybe later.

THERESA No. Tell me now.

MERCER Well, I just, I want to write about how men and
women see each other, but obviously I'm not qualified to
write about this from a woman's perspective. I mean, I can
guess, but I don't really know how women perceive themselves. In relation to the ways in which men perceive them.
If you know what I mean.

THERESA I do.

MERCER So that's where I would need your help. *(*THERESA
doesn't answer.)* Or your blessing. *(She still doesn't answer.)* Or something. *(She picks up the letter.)*

THERESA Here are the ways in which I perceive myself, in relation to the ways men perceive me: I perceive myself to be
a bitch.

MERCER Don't read that.

THERESA I perceive myself as something to be fucked until I scream.

MERCER *(Putting down the phone)* This isn't what I meant.

THERESA *(Overlapping with "meant")* As something to be nailed to the ground and fucked so hard I split in two.

MERCER Theresa, please don't look at that.

THERESA As something to be fucked where I'm small. I don't even know what that means. Something to be fucked where I'm small.

MERCER *(In spite of himself)* I think he means . . . sodomized.

THERESA Then add that to your list.

MERCER *(Holding out his hand for the letter)* Don't keep looking at that. This isn't what I meant.

THERESA My life is not theoretical.

MERCER I know.

THERESA You don't get to make something theoretical out of my life.

MERCER *(Taking a step toward her)* Theresa. Please. Stop.

THERESA *(She backs away.)* No, you stop.

MERCER Okay. *(He backs off.)*

THERESA You stop.

MERCER Okay. *(He moves back to the phone, picks it up.)* I'm still on hold.

THERESA I'm not theoretical. I'm real.

Scene three

Theresa's office, the following day. THERESA *is talking to* DE-
TECTIVE BECK. *She is wearing the same clothes.*

BECK Have you gotten any more letters?

THERESA No.

BECK Phone calls?

THERESA None here, but he might have called me at home. I
spent last night at my boss's place. I didn't want to be by
myself.

BECK Can you stay there for a while?

THERESA I guess so. I also called my friend Linda. She lives
out on Long Island. She says I can stay with her for as long
as I like. But he knows where she lives, so I didn't know.

BECK I'd stay where you are for now, if you're comfortable.
That way your boss can go with you to and from work. You
should take a cab every night and have the driver sort of
drive you around first.

(Beat.)

THERESA What's wrong?

BECK I can't find your guy.

THERESA What?

BECK He moved out of his apartment last week, and when I
went by his work, they told me he'd been fired over two
months ago. I couldn't get the woman to talk at first, but
when I told her why I was there, she let me know that he
was fired for activity just like this.

THERESA He was stalking somebody?

BECK Yeah. Somebody where he worked. The woman's been transferred. They wouldn't say where. But this is sort of what I was wondering. If maybe he'd been stalking somebody and she evaded him so he was just looking for somebody else to fixate on.

THERESA So I'm just an understudy.

BECK So to speak. But to him, now, it's you he's fixated on.

THERESA He doesn't even have a job?

BECK No.

THERESA So he can stalk me full-time?

BECK Yeah. Try not to be alone. Try not to go anywhere that's not absolutely necessary. *(Beat.)* He might have gotten out all he wanted to say to you in the letter.

THERESA Do you think?

BECK I don't know. *(Handing her an envelope from her bag)* Here. I got a copy of his picture, from his work ID. You should show it to security here, at your boss's place. Let them know to keep an eye out for the guy.

THERESA *(Doesn't open the envelope.)* I don't want to look at him.

BECK Just do it sooner rather than later, okay?

THERESA *(Putting the envelope in her drawer)* Okay. *(Beat.)* How long have you done this?

BECK I've worked on this particular detail for two years now. I worked in a rape response unit before that.

THERESA Doesn't it depress you?

BECK It does, but it also makes me feel good about myself, that I can be of some help to people.

THERESA Is there a pattern? In these cases?

BECK There are some profiles for stalkers, whether it's a man or a woman—

THERESA No, I mean, the people who are stalked. Is there anything about them?

BECK No. I don't know. They come from all walks of life.

THERESA *(Beat.)* Do they train you on how to talk to people like me?

BECK They do.

THERESA Because I feel like you have a standard way of talking. I mean, your language. The way you phrase things.

BECK There are standard procedures. I like to think, though, that I respond to people as individuals. In individual ways.

THERESA I'm not criticizing you. I find it kind of comforting. That there's a standard reply to this. It means I'm not alone.

BECK Right.

THERESA But do I seem like a person who would get stalked?

BECK No. There's never any rhyme or reason to it. It's never anybody's fault.

THERESA I keep thinking I did something.

BECK That's only because you're human.

THERESA I am?

BECK *(Smiles.)* Yeah. *(Small beat.)* That's not really what I mean, though. I just mean . . . like I'm from this big family. Five boys and I'm the only girl, and my parents paid for my brothers to go to college. But they never even offered to pay for me, because I was supposed to get married right out of high school. I was engaged and everything, and the guy I was supposed to marry, he won a Pulitzer Prize last year.

THERESA Who is he?

BECK I don't want to tell you.

THERESA Who does he write for?

BECK It's not important. I didn't want to marry him. That's all that matters. I went to Hunter College instead, and I had to pay my own way because my family thought I was making such a huge mistake.

THERESA Does he write for the *Times*?

BECK It doesn't matter. My point is that I had to work my way through college. But why? Why didn't I demand that my parents pay my tuition? They paid for my brothers. Right? So why didn't I demand that they pay for me?

THERESA I don't know.

BECK Because it didn't occur to me. Because the system of my family and the system of the world around my family never laid out that option for me, and so I never thought of it.

THERESA I don't understand the connection.

BECK Just that we can't always tell how much is us and how much is the world around us. *(Small beat.)* If that makes any sense.

THERESA Okay. When I was a freshman in college, I dated a guy who was a bartender. I would go and sit at the bar and wait for him to get off work. And there was this old man there who was always drinking alone and I always felt sorry for him. One night, he started talking to me, telling me all about his life and how he had lost his wife and how his children didn't speak to him anymore, and I felt really sorry for him and I told him I felt bad for him and he told me it would make him feel better to kiss a pretty girl. So I let him kiss me. On the mouth. *(Beat.)* I didn't want to at all. He was an old drunk and it made me sick. But I did it anyway because it's what I thought I was supposed to do. I was supposed to be nice. *(Beat.)* And then later that year, I was covering a Take Back the Night Rally for the school paper, and this woman turned to me and saw me taking notes, and she asked me if I was there as a reporter, or as a woman, and I said as a reporter, and she was disgusted. She wanted a protester, not a reporter. But I didn't want to say as a woman, because I hadn't had many good experiences as a woman, so when she presented me with another option, I jumped at it. *(Beat.)* Maybe being a woman, to me, meant tolerating a lot of shit. And maybe I never learned otherwise. I still tolerate shit, but I do it as a reporter, so it just seems like part of the job. But maybe it's really still me thinking that's what I'm supposed to do, as a woman. Sit and listen to some asshole go on and on about himself, and then reward him for it. So maybe that's why I told Tony that it was entirely me, when that wasn't the truth. It was actually entirely him. *(Beat.)* Is that what you were saying?

BECK Um . . . I don't know. I think so.

THERESA I think it was. *(Beat.)* I'm glad you didn't marry that guy.

BECK Thanks. *(Beat. She stands.)* Okay, then. I'll call you as soon as I know something.

THERESA Okay.

BECK I know it's hard, but try not to worry. *(*THERESA *nods.* BECK *studies her.)* Come here.

THERESA What?

BECK Just come here.

*(*BECK *gives* THERESA *a big hug.* THERESA *is surprised at first, then very grateful as she relaxes into it.)*

Scene four

Theresa's office. HARRIET *enters.*

THERESA Do you need something, Harriet?

HARRIET Howard told me what was going on, with Tony, and I am so sorry.

THERESA Oh. Well, thank you.

HARRIET He just wanted me to know. I noticed how you'd been wearing the same clothes the last three days.

THERESA Yeah, I guess I have.

HARRIET So I was thinking, maybe you'd like to go out to lunch and then maybe go over to Saks. Tish Cornwall is doing a demonstration. She has a new line of makeup, and she and her team are giving free makeovers. It might be fun.

THERESA I don't think I can.

HARRIET I just thought, you know, because of what was going on with you, maybe it'd be nice to treat yourself to something. If I had the money, I'd offer to treat you to a day at the salon. That's what my mom would do.

THERESA Really.

HARRIET Yeah. When I was in high school, if I ever had anything really upsetting happen to me, she'd take me down for the works. I loved it. All the old ladies there would go on and on about how pretty I was, and I'd order everybody around. Make them bring me juice.

THERESA I'm sure it was fun.

HARRIET It was. *(Beat.)* I just thought, maybe if you pampered yourself a little bit. I'm a big believer in being good to yourself.

THERESA Harriet, I'm afraid I'll have to pass. I feel kind of funny walking around, and, I don't know, sort of the last thing I want to do right now is get a makeover. But thank you anyway.

HARRIET Can I do anything else for you?

THERESA Um . . . well, you could, actually. But, if this makes you uncomfortable, just say so, okay? I need to go back to my apartment and get some things, but in the meantime, I could really use some underwear. If you're going to Saks anyway . . .

HARRIET Sure.

THERESA Are you sure?

HARRIET I'm positive.

THERESA *(Getting money from her wallet)* You can just get me the kind that comes in the packs. Um, I like all cotton.

HARRIET What size? Five?

THERESA I think six.

HARRIET I bet you're a five.

THERESA Go ahead and get a six. I'd rather have them too big.

HARRIET God, me too. *(She takes the money.)*

THERESA Thank you so much, Harriet.

HARRIET It's no problem.

THERESA I know, but it's not something I would ever normally ask you to do. Buy underwear for your boss.

HARRIET I promise I don't mind. *(Beat.)* You look terrible.

THERESA Thanks.

HARRIET No. God, I'm sorry. I just meant, that if there's anything else, let me know. *(MERCER enters.)* Hey.

MERCER *(Looks at her.)* How do you walk in those shoes?

HARRIET They're tall, but they're flat. *(To THERESA)* I'll be back around two.

THERESA Take your time.

(HARRIET exits).

MERCER Where's she going?

THERESA Lunch.

MERCER She's supposed to . . . *(He turns, she's gone.)* She was supposed to do some *work* this morning. *(Beat.)* Can I talk to you?

THERESA Sure.

MERCER Look, I know that I handled this whole thing very badly. I was insensitive and pushy when I shouldn't have been, but . . .

THERESA But?

MERCER When you first asked me to listen to those mes-

sages, I honestly wasn't thinking, Oh, here's a story. I was
thinking that someone I like and respect was in trouble and
that she seemed to need my help. That's all. But when that
policewoman came in here and started to talk, I thought,
My God, there's a standard protocol here, and that made
me wonder what else is standard? A standard personality?
A standard play of events? And I couldn't help but be curi-
ous then. And I wanted to write about it. But I handled it
very badly, and I'm sorry for that.

THERESA But?

MERCER But I'm still writing the story.

THERESA I figured you were. *(Beat.)* Look, I thought all that,
too. When I could think again. So I don't blame you for
wanting to write the article. But right now I don't think I
want to read it.

MERCER I wasn't going to ask you to. And thank you. *(Small
beat.)* So you've been staying at Howard's?

THERESA Yeah. *(Beat.)* He's the hugest slob I've ever seen in
my whole life. I had no idea. His bathtub has an inch of
brown gunk on the bottom. I was sitting on the toilet, I
looked at it, and I thought I'd throw up. I already had diar-
rhea and I thought it would come out the other end, too.

MERCER I'm sorry.

THERESA I can't believe I just told you that. I'm sorry.

MERCER It's okay.

THERESA Sometimes I don't know what's coming out of my
own mouth. I feel like I do . . . you know when you're trying to pack for a long trip and you just keep walking
around your apartment with, like a blow-dryer in your

hand, and you're not really packing anything? You're just walking around? I feel like that.

MERCER You're under a lot of pressure.

THERESA Everybody's noticed, haven't they? That I've been wearing the same clothes.

MERCER A couple of people did. I told them your apartment burned up.

THERESA You did?

MERCER Yeah.

THERESA Thanks.

MERCER You know, if you don't feel like going back to your place, I'd be happy to pick some things up for you. If you just tell me what you need.

THERESA Maybe so.

(Beat.)

MERCER If it would make you more comfortable, I could ask Howard to come with me.

THERESA Mercer, don't take it personally. It's not you. I just . . . I don't feel comfortable going back myself right now, but for some reason I don't want anybody else there either.

MERCER I understand. But let me know if you change your mind. Or you think of anything else. *(He starts to leave.)*

THERESA Would you mind . . . would you like to sit down and talk for a while?

MERCER Sure. Of course.

THERESA It's no big deal, I just— I've been feeling lonely lately.

MERCER I'm sorry.

THERESA It's no big deal.

(Small beat.)

MERCER So what would you like to talk about?

THERESA I don't know. Why don't you tell me about your wife? How long have you been together?

MERCER Sixteen years. We met in college.

THERESA Did you both like Aerosmith?

MERCER *(Laughs.)* No, we met . . . well, we met at a dance. We both got stood up.

THERESA Oh no.

MERCER Yeah. Michelle had a date with a rugby player and he got drunk and passed out before the dance. And I had a date with this woman from my poetry class. I thought she was great. She was always quoting "The Wasteland" and smoking clove cigarettes and she seemed really tragic and beautiful. So before the dance I went out and—this is so embarrassing, but I actually bought a beret.

THERESA Oh God.

MERCER Yeah. And that night, I spent about an hour getting it situated on my head and, you know, arranging my hair around it. And then I got to the dance and my tragic beauty wasn't there. So I waited. And I waited and waited even though I knew she wasn't coming because that was the tragic thing to do. But then after a while I noticed there was this really cute girl in a green dress, and she was also waiting and waiting. So I went up to her and asked her to dance, and she smiled, and there was nothing tragic in that smile. So I took off the beret and we danced.

THERESA That's so sweet.

MERCER Yeah. Sometimes I want to find that girl from my poetry class and write her a check for not showing up.

(Beat.)

THERESA When I got ready to go out to dinner with him, that Saturday night, I changed clothes three times. I kept looking at myself in the mirror.

MERCER You were nervous.

THERESA No, it's more . . . I was looking in the mirror . . . I was looking in the mirror to see how I would look to him. *(Beat.)* When I think about that now, it makes me physically ill.

MERCER You didn't know.

THERESA It makes me physically ill. How much I wanted to look good.

Scene five

Les Kennkat's hospital room. LES *is propped up in bed. A few flowers are around. The curtain that separates his bed from his roommate's is drawn and his roommate is hidden. He is awake, not doing anything.* HOWARD *and* THERESA *enter.*

THERESA Here we are.

HOWARD I'll be down the hall. *(Exits.)*

LES You came!

THERESA I did.

LES Who was that?

THERESA My editor. Howard.

LES He can come in.

THERESA He's going to go get a Coke.

(Beat.)

LES You came!

THERESA I did. How are you?

LES Good. Good. They took my colon out.

THERESA Do you have a . . . bag thing now?

LES A colostomy bag?

THERESA Right.

LES No. They attached my lower intestine directly to my rectum.

THERESA Oh.

LES I didn't think you'd come.

THERESA I didn't know you were so sick. So when you called, I guess I felt bad. I don't know. I don't know why I came.

LES You felt sorry for me.

THERESA I guess.

LES It's all right if it got you down here. I sent you flowers, but they came back. They said you refused delivery.

THERESA I didn't know.

LES You didn't refuse?

THERESA Well, I did. But it's a blanket refusal. It wasn't meant for you, really.

LES You're just morally opposed to flowers?

THERESA It's a long story. Why'd you send me flowers?

LES To thank you! For the article! It was brilliant.

THERESA It was?

LES Yes. I've never had a better write-up. You captured the quintessential me. Again and again, Les Kennkat, a lover of large breasts. I couldn't have done it better myself. Three days later I had backers for my new movie, and then this kid from MTV called and wants to know, do I want to host some special—they want to call it *Girls Are Go!*—all about the era, the girls, the retro hip kitsch thing with girls in go-go boots and the vinyl miniskirts, dancing in cages and all that. You were right! I am a cult hero. So I sent you the flowers as a thank you, but when they came back, I thought maybe you were angry and I wanted to find out why and set it straight, because I'm a man who repays his obligations and I am now, officially, obliged to you.

THERESA You don't have to thank me. I was just doing my job.

LES Then you're not angry?

THERESA No. I don't know. Maybe you can't help being a jerk.

LES I can't. As hard as I try, I can't.

THERESA Maybe it's generational.

LES It could be.

THERESA Or genetic.

LES Or bluff.

THERESA What?

LES A man's gotta make a living.

THERESA There are other ways to make a living.

LES Not for me. I'm not talented. I'm not smart. I'm just fear-
less.

THERESA Or shameless.

LES Or shameless.

(Beat.)

THERESA Well, I have to go. Howard's waiting for me.

LES Aw, do you have to? I've been sitting here all day by myself.

THERESA I guess I can stay a minute.

LES Good. It's spooky here, it's so quiet. I think the guy in the
next bed is dead. He never says a word.

THERESA *(Peeking behind the curtain)* He's not dead.

LES What is he? A vegetable?

THERESA I think he's comatose. Yes.

LES They keep going behind that curtain with little bags and
tubes. I figured he was a vegetable. Hospitals are very depressing places.

THERESA Who sent the flowers?

LES My producers.

THERESA Do you have any family?

LES No.

THERESA Me neither. To speak of.

LES You never married?

THERESA No.

LES I was married.

THERESA I know. Joy Box.

LES Kathy. Kathy was her real name. *(Beat.)* That was the
biggest mistake I ever made in my life.

THERESA Getting married?

LES No. Losing Kathy.

(Pause.)

THERESA Well. I should go . . .

LES Are you sure you can't stay? The nurses tell me that chair's pretty comfortable. And *Jeopardy!* is coming on. It's no fun watching it by yourself, if you can't impress anybody with how smart you are.

THERESA You're not going to ask me to kiss you, are you?

LES No. Why would I do that?

THERESA I don't know. It's something old men do sometimes.

LES I promise. That was bluff and bluster for the press. To-day you're not working. You're here as a visitor only. Okay? A visiting friend.

THERESA Well, I kind of feel like staying.

LES Then stay.

THERESA Okay.

(She sits. LES *picks up the remote.)*

LES I'm not sure how this thing works. I pressed a button here and the sound went away, and then I pressed another and everything was in Spanish. *(He tries to work the re-mote.)* See, I want Channel 9. In English.

THERESA Can I try?

LES Please. *(He hands her the remote.* THERESA *pushes some buttons, the sound of* Jeopardy! *comes on faintly.)* That's it! Put that thing on the table now, and don't touch it. I don't want it messed up again. *(*THERESA *puts down the re-mote.)* Good timing! It's just starting. *(Beat. They watch TV.)* We can watch the whole thing.

Theresa's office. THERESA *and* MERCER *enter, talking.* THERESA *is wearing the same pants, but a man's shirt.*

THERESA He's okay, I guess. It was funny. We watched *Jeopardy!* And he didn't know even the easiest ones. But then, when he did know one, he got so excited, like a little kid. Just so proud of himself. And then he told me he never graduated from high school. That when he was a kid, when he was fourteen, it was during the Depression, and one day his father came to him and told him he had to leave the house. That they didn't have enough food for the whole family and he was the oldest so he would just have to go out and make it on his own. He said he sat in the back yard and cried. And then he went inside and packed a bag and went down to the rail yards and figured out how to hop a freight, and that's what he did for the next three years. He hopped freights and went from town to town and lived like a bum. He said he was lonely and scared all the time. He said he met a girl once, in a town, and he thought she was the prettiest, nicest person he'd ever met, and she agreed to walk with him in the park, but her mother caught them and had him arrested. Just because he was poor.

MERCER That's terrible.

THERESA I know. And I thought, if girls were this unattainable thing to him, this prize that he didn't deserve, then sure, he would go on to make movies about breasts in trees.

MERCER I suppose.

THERESA You can understand somebody without excusing them. (HARRIET *enters with a little gift bag.*) Not again.

HARRIET Mercer, you have a call on line three.

MERCER Thanks. (*He exits.*)

THERESA Harriet. You have to stop buying me presents.

HARRIET They're just little treats. To cheer you up. (THERESA *pulls a little bottle of cologne out of the bag.*) It's what I wear. You complimented it one day.

THERESA (*Takes off the cap, smells it.*) It's nice. But you should keep it for yourself.

HARRIET No.

THERESA I know you don't make any money.

HARRIET It's okay. I put it on my mother's card.

THERESA Then that's double the reason. I don't want your mother buying me presents.

HARRIET But that's why she gave me the card. She wanted me to use it for just this thing: treats.

THERESA All right, Harriet. Thank you. But no more.

HARRIET I can't promise that.

(HOWARD *enters. His pants are ripped at the knee and his knee is scraped.*)

HARRIET Oh my God! What happened?

THERESA (*Overlapping*) Howard!

HOWARD I fell down.

THERESA Are you okay?

HOWARD I'm fine. Listen, this guy, Tony, what does he look like?

THERESA Tall. Brown hair. Fairly thin. Why?

HOWARD *(To Harriet)* Harriet? Can you get me something for my knee? *(Harriet exits.)* I thought I saw this guy yesterday. At lunch. A young guy sitting across from me and Jim Watkins. And I thought he was staring at me, but I tried not to be paranoid. Then this morning there was that reception for Carrie Banks, over at the *Post*, she's retiring. It was a huge thing, and I swear this same guy was there, standing in the corner, sort of. Staring at me again. So I just went up to him. And I said, "Do I know you from somewhere or do you know me?" And he said it was neither. I was mistaken. And then I felt like an idiot. But then, when I was leaving, I saw him going for his coat, like he was going to follow me. So I ran out a side door and down the alley. Like I was Harrison Ford or something. But when I looked back, he was coming out the door, too. He was following me. So I ran out in the street and flagged down a cab. I was so nervous, trying to get to it, I tripped and fell.

THERESA Howard . . .

HOWARD I'm okay. But by the time I got up, the guy was gone. *(Laughs nervously.)* That cabbie must've thought I was crazy.

THERESA *(Remembering, opening her drawer)* Wait a minute, the police gave me a picture.

(She hands him the envelope. HOWARD *pulls out the picture.)*

HOWARD That's him. *(He hands it back to her.* THERESA *looks at it for the first time.)* What do you think he wants?

THERESA I don't know. Oh my God, if he did anything to you . . .

HOWARD *(Overlapping)* Hey, hey. Don't worry about me.

THERESA I'll call Detective Beck. *(Starts looking for the number in her Rolodex.)*

HOWARD Why do you think he's following me?

THERESA I wonder if he's seen us together.

HOWARD I don't think he could have followed us home. But if he's seen us come into the building together, maybe he's figured out that you're staying with me.

THERESA I was so hoping he'd gone away. I was even thinking about going back to my apartment.

HOWARD You can't do that.

THERESA I know. But I miss my things. I'd like to have some of my clothes at least.

HOWARD What, you don't like my shirt?

THERESA *(Fingers her shirt.)* When did you buy this?

HOWARD It's Brooks Brothers. It never goes out of style.

THERESA I just miss my things.

HOWARD Look, ask the police, and if they think it's okay, Mercer and I will go and pack up some stuff for you.

THERESA Okay.

HOWARD I got a meeting upstairs at two, so if that cop comes by before then, see if she'll wait.

THERESA All right.

HOWARD *(Looks at his pants.)* These are my best pants.

THERESA Thank you, Howard.

HOWARD For what?

THERESA Just . . . for everything.

HOWARD Hell.

*(*HOWARD *exits.* THERESA *picks up the phone and dials.)*

THERESA Can I speak to Detective Beck, please?

*(*MERCER *enters with* HARRIET *right behind him.)*

MERCER Howard says he saw Tony. *(Sees she's on the phone.)* Sorry.

THERESA *(On phone)* Could you ask her to call Theresa Bedell, please? She has my number . . . Thanks.

MERCER What happened?

THERESA He was following Howard.

HARRIET Oh God! Is that why he's bleeding?

THERESA He's okay, Harriet, don't panic.

HARRIET Oh God. Theresa . . . I have to tell you something really private. Mercer, will you leave?

MERCER *(Looks to* THERESA, *who nods.)* Sure.

*(*MERCER *exits.* HARRIET *closes the door.)*

HARRIET I am so sorry.

THERESA Why?

HARRIET I am so sorry.

THERESA Harriet.

HARRIET I didn't know. I mean, I just thought, you know, you had broken up with your boyfriend and Tony seemed so nice and everything. I didn't know you at all. And then, in all honesty, you seemed sort of mad or mean or something at first. I mean, not mean, but you didn't really tell me anything and he kept calling and I had to deal with him and one day—he called to see if you'd gotten some flowers— and I said you wouldn't take his call and he started crying, and he sounded so sad, so I told him, I knew how he felt, you know? If he wanted to talk. *(Beat.)* And then he really opened up to me. I thought. He really seemed to trust me.

THERESA What did you tell him?

HARRIET He just wanted to tell you how much he loved you. He said. *(Beat.)* I gave him your home phone number. And then, when you kept wearing the same clothes to work . . . I think I may have told him that you weren't living at your apartment anymore.

THERESA That's why you've been buying me all the presents.

HARRIET Yes.

THERESA How many times did you talk to him?

HARRIET I don't know. A lot. I guess. But after I found out, I didn't talk to him again. I swear! I told him I knew what he was doing and I wouldn't talk to him again and he stopped calling. I swear.

THERESA When was that?

HARRIET Like, a week ago?

(Pause.)

THERESA Okay, Harriet. Thank you for telling me. I know that was hard to do . . .

HARRIET I'm so sorry.

THERESA But in spite of that, you're fired.

HARRIET But I'm sorry.

THERESA You're also fired.

HARRIET Oh my God.

(Pause. HARRIET looks as if she will cry. THERESA holds out the cologne.)

THERESA Here.

HARRIET I bought it for you.

THERESA But you need a treat right now.

Scene seven

Theresa's apartment; night. It has been ransacked. Books, papers, clothes are everywhere. Everything is ripped up. Pages are torn from books. The furniture is overturned, the futon gutted. A jangling of keys from outside, then the door opens slightly.

HOWARD *(From offstage)* I don't think it was locked.

MERCER *(From offstage)* Watch out.

(HOWARD *slowly pushes the door open. He and* MERCER *are both carrying an empty box. They look at the apartment.)*

HOWARD Oh God. *(He takes a step inside.)*

MERCER Wait a minute! *(He grabs* HOWARD. *They stand, unsure what to do.)* Do you have your phone with you?

HOWARD I gave it to Theresa.

MERCER Okay. *(Yells)* We're coming in! We're coming in the door!

HOWARD Oh, great. Now he knows where to find us.

MERCER *(Yells)* We're armed!

HOWARD No, we're not.

MERCER *(Yells)* It's the police! Whoever's in here, come out with your hands up!

(Beat. Nothing happens.)

HOWARD He's not here.

MERCER I smell something.

HOWARD *(Sniffs.)* Something rotten.

MERCER I'm calling the police. *(He picks up the phone and sees it's been ripped from the wall.)*

HOWARD Hang on. *(He goes in, walks down the hall. From offstage we hear him.)* Aw jeez.

MERCER What? What? Are you okay? *(Long pause. Nothing happens.* MERCER *jumps at nothing.)* Howard?! *(No answer.)* Howard!

HOWARD *(Enters.)* There's only three rooms here.

MERCER What is it?

HOWARD He's not here. The kitchen is wrecked. There's food everywhere, roaches. That's what you smell. *(Looks at his fingers.)* I put my hand in something.

MERCER What?

HOWARD *(Smells his hand.)* Shampoo. It's all over the bath. *(He picks up a shirt lying on the floor. It's been ripped to shreds.)* Look at this. He couldn't just go through everything, he had to ruin it, too.

*(*MERCER *steps gingerly into the middle of the room, looks around.)*

MERCER What do you think he was after?

HOWARD I don't know.

MERCER It took a long time to do this.

HOWARD No kidding. *(Small beat.)* Thanks for coming with me.

MERCER Thanks for coming with *me.*

HOWARD We probably shouldn't touch anything, huh?

MERCER Well, it's not like we don't know who did it.

HOWARD True. Do you think we could find some clothes that aren't ruined, at least? So we can take *something* back to her? Let's not tell her exactly what happened. Let's just say we couldn't bring anything back because the police wouldn't let us. Let's not tell her it's all torn up like this.

MERCER She's going to have to know sometime.

HOWARD But not now. She's too upset, I can tell. She's not sleeping. I never see her eat.

MERCER It's really good of you to let her stay with you.

HOWARD It's great for me. My apartment's never been so clean. She's run out of things to scrub. The other morning, I came in, she'd been up all night arranging my books. By genre and by author. *(Beat.)* Also, I sort of like the company. After my mother died, I thought I didn't want another roommate. But it's not so bad.

MERCER You lived with your mother?

HOWARD Yeah. She was ill. After my wife and I split up, I moved her in with me.

MERCER I didn't know you were married.

HOWARD Seven years. *(They look around for a moment.)* What a mess. *(Beat.)* I've never been in her apartment before. Have you?

MERCER No.

HOWARD *(They start looking, gingerly picking through things.)* Yeah, after we split up, my mother moved in. You know, my wife, she initiated the split up or separation or whatever. She was unhappy. A lot of things weren't working out. I should have seen it coming, but I didn't. I mean, in retrospect, I understand entirely, but at the time it really took me by surprise. It kind of made me gun-shy. Around women. It didn't show, I don't think, but I had friends who'd try and fix me up with dates and I always made excuses. My mom was sick. I had to work. But basically, I didn't trust anybody. *(Beat.)* Sometimes I'd fantasize I was yelling at my wife.

MERCER What was her name?

HOWARD Claudia.

MERCER What would you say?

HOWARD "Claudia! What do you expect me to do? Read your mind? How am I supposed to know what you want when you won't tell me?"

MERCER Maybe she didn't know herself.

HOWARD She didn't.

(They look around.)

MERCER Last year, last New Year's Eve, my wife dragged us to ten different bars. We had to go here, we had to go there. Nothing was quite right. This one was too crowded, this one too empty, this one had cheesy music. We spent most of the night in cabs. Finally I said, "What's the matter? What do you want?" She said she didn't know. She just felt restless and sad. Our best friends had moved out to L.A. We always used to spend New Year's with them. She was feeling lonely.

HOWARD At least she didn't turn to you and say, "All I know is I don't want to be with you."

MERCER No. That wasn't it. Thank God. *(Leans over, picks* *up a calendar.)* She has a cat calendar. Does she have a cat?

HOWARD   I don't think so.

MERCER   *(Flipping through the calendar.)* What's this?

HOWARD   What?

MERCER   She's got it every month. A little dot with a circle around it.

HOWARD   I don't know.

MERCER   Different days, once a month. What does that mean?

HOWARD   Payday?

MERCER   No. *(Looking. Beat.* HOWARD *picks up a book.)* Oh.

HOWARD   What?

MERCER   It's her period. It must be . . . when her period starts. *(They are very uncomfortable. They look around.)*

HOWARD   This isn't a good idea, I don't think. Let's just leave this stuff here and call the cops.

MERCER   How could he even think of this. I would never think of this.

HOWARD   Me neither. Just "Claudia, what do you want?" Just stuff like that.

(Pause.)

MERCER   I thought about Theresa once.

HOWARD   What do you mean?

MERCER   About a month after I started work. I still didn't know her well. You asked me to edit some freelance stuff and I didn't know what I was doing and she gave me some suggestions, and she was standing by her desk, sort of leaning on it. She was wearing what she always wears, slacks and a jacket, it wasn't anything she was doing or wearing, but I just looked at her and I thought, I want to fuck her. Right then, I could just . . . I wanted to close the door to her office and . . . fuck her. I guess I imagined she'd be willing, I mean, I wasn't thinking of jumping on her . . .

HOWARD Sure, sure.

MERCER I mean, I've never cheated on Michelle and I never will. I don't want to. It wasn't—it was just one of those things that flashes through your mind. I mean now, I can't even imagine it.

HOWARD You didn't make a move . . .

MERCER No. Of course not. I never would.

HOWARD Then it's harmless.

MERCER I guess. *(Beat.)* I don't know.

HOWARD *(They put down the things they're holding and start to leave.)* So how does this fit in?

MERCER With what?

HOWARD With your theory. The guy watches the girl, the guy gets the girl. What's this?

MERCER *(Looks around.)* The guy hurts the girl.

Scene eight

Theresa's office, the next day. She and OFFICER BECK *are talking.*

BECK *(Handing her a card)* That's got a 1-800 number on it, so you can reach me from wherever.

THERESA *(Taking it, looking at it)* Thanks. M. Beck?

BECK Madeleine.

THERESA Thanks, Madeleine.

BECK Take care of yourself.

THERESA You too.

(BECK *exits.* MERCER *is waiting outside, and he and* BECK *exchange nods as he comes in.)*

MERCER What'd she say?

THERESA They found another letter in my apartment. In the medicine cabinet. They think he wanted me to find it when I was alone. He said he wants to put a wire around my throat and pull it until it . . . until it slices through my throat.

MERCER Jesus.

THERESA There were other details, but I chose not to hear them.

MERCER Well, what are they going to do?

THERESA They'll put out a warrant for his arrest, but they probably won't find him unless he messes up somehow and draws attention to himself.

MERCER Unless he tries to attack you.

THERESA Pretty much, yeah.

MERCER Jesus.

THERESA It's not her fault. She has a million cases.

MERCER A million?

THERESA A hundred. It may as well be a million. *(Beat.)* You know—

MERCER *(Overlapping)* Theresa, I'm not—*(Stops.)* Sorry, go ahead.

THERESA No, you go ahead.

MERCER Um, I'm not going to write my story after all. About what's been going on. I'm sorry I ever suggested it. It was wrong.

THERESA Are you sure?

MERCER Yeah. So what were you going to say? Before?

THERESA *(Picks up the magazine.)* Did you read my article about the Yankees?

MERCER I did. I liked it.

THERESA Apparently it's pretty good. I don't even know what I wrote.

MERCER It is good. I read it on the train this morning. It actually made me want to watch the World Series. And I hate baseball.

THERESA Well, you're not the only one who liked it. The editor of the *Denver Free Press* called me this morning. I kind of know him. I met him at a conference last year, and he told me then, if I ever wanted a job, to call him. But I didn't, so I forgot about it. But he called today and he said he read the story and that he wanted to make an offer again. That he needs a new sports columnist, and he thinks I'd be great at it. So I told him I'd think about it.

MERCER You did?

THERESA I told him as long as all he wanted was a woman. You know, as long as he didn't want me, because I'd have to write under another name—

MERCER You can't move to Denver.

THERESA And he said that he would rather it be me, you know, under my own name, but that he understood and

I could use any name I wanted. That what he wanted
was me, but he'd take a woman if he couldn't have
me—

MERCER What are you going to do in Denver?

THERESA I'm going to get an apartment and I'm going to live
in it. I'm going to walk around outside.

MERCER It's not right.

THERESA What's the difference? Why should I wait around
until he decides to kill me?

MERCER But he'll win.

THERESA He's already won. Whatever it was he wanted me to
feel, I feel it.

MERCER You're terrified.

THERESA No, it's more than that *(Beat.)* It's like when I go
running in the park . . . if I still could . . . every week or so,
not every day, but every week or two some guy drives by or
walks by and says something to me. You know, "Nice ass"
or "I want to jog with you" or "Fuck you." Or "Fuck me."
It's been happening since I was twelve, so I know how to
ignore it. But every tenth time or so, I still feel it. I feel re-
duced. I feel like everything that I know about myself—that
I'm a good writer and I've read a lot of books, and . . . I like
fall better than spring or . . . I haven't had many friends really since my parents died, even though that was a long
time ago—everything I know about myself, just gets wiped
out. It's like I'm just this thing running down the sidewalk.
I'm not me anymore. I'm just this thing. *(Beat.)* And that's
how I feel now. All the time.

(Long pause.)

MERCER Well, one thing I can tell you . . . I'm your friend. I
see you and I know it's you. I know you're there. I do.

THERESA I know. *(Small beat.)* It's not enough.

Scene nine

Theresa's apartment, a week later. It is night; a light is on.
THERESA *and* MERCER *are going through what's left of her*
things. A big pile of trash is in one corner, some boxes with
books are scattered about. THERESA *is picking through a pile of*
torn-up paperbacks. MERCER *is looking through books as well.*

THERESA So he called me yesterday, because they'd filmed
the MTV thing and he was so excited. I guess they treated
him like royalty and everybody thought he was a riot. But
he said that when he got to the studios, they took him into
this big dressing room and there was this huge spread, just
for him, with cookies and sandwich stuff and everything,
and he started crying.

MERCER Poor guy.

THERESA No, he started crying because he's on a special diet,
because of his colon, and he couldn't touch any of it.

MERCER *(Laughs.)* Oh. Hey, do you want this *Access New*
York?

THERESA No. Keep it if you want it.

MERCER Thanks.

THERESA *(Throwing a bunch of books on the trash pile)* He
ripped up all my Shakespeare.

MERCER He hates the Bard.

THERESA He ripped up all my pictures. My parents' wedding photos. But he took all the pictures of me. *(Beat.)* I had an old box of letters under the bed, though. He didn't find those.

MERCER I'll send you a Riverside Shakespeare. All in one big book.

THERESA *(Smiles.)* Thanks.

MERCER So anyway, Les is flying you out . . .

THERESA Right. I told him I was leaving town and why, and he just made this weird noise and said he had to go and hung up. And I was really upset for a minute. It hurt my feelings. But then he called back five minutes later and he had called one of these producers on his new movie, and the guy has a private plane and Les arranged to have him fly me to Denver.

MERCER That's nice.

THERESA I know. He also intimated that he has ties to the Mafia and if I wanted Tony's knees broken, all I had to do was say the word. (MERCER *picks up an intact book and opens it.)* So Linda's picking me up tonight to take me out to her place for the night, and then tomorrow I'm doing the name-change thing, so I can do everything in Denver with my new name, and then Linda and Chris are taking me to the airport tomorrow night.

MERCER *(Still looking at the book)* Uh-huh.

(HOWARD *enters, carrying a pot and a pan.)*

HOWARD Mercer.

MERCER What?

HOWARD This is what she has in her kitchen. One pot and one pan.

THERESA I don't cook.

HOWARD *(Throwing the pot and pan in a box)* There. I packed your kitchen.

THERESA Good. Now do the bathroom. *(HOWARD exits. MERCER throws the book he was looking at in the trash pile.)* What's wrong with that one?

MERCER You don't want it.

THERESA I do, too, what is it? *(Fetching it) The Culture of Narcissism.* I do, too.

MERCER *(Taking it from her)* You don't want it.

THERESA There's nothing wrong with it.

MERCER He wrote in it.

THERESA What?

MERCER He wrote in the margins. There are gross things in the margins. *(THERESA looks, reads, quickly closes it. MERCER takes it and throws it in the trash pile.)* Maybe we should check the other ones.

THERESA All of these . . . ? *(She pulls a book from the box, opens it, flips, stops.)* Oh God. *(She starts pulling books from the box. Same thing.)* How long . . . how long was he in here doing this? *(She shoves the box away.)* Goddammit!

MERCER Leave it all. Even if it's okay, you're going to know he touched it and it's not worth it. Leave it all.

(THERESA looks around.)

THERESA Oh God. My letters. *(She opens the box and pulls* *out a letter.)* If he . . . *(She pulls a letter out and begins to read it. The buzzer sounds.)*

MERCER That must be Linda. *(Into buzzer)* Hello? *(No answer.)*

THERESA *(Flipping the letter over)* I don't think he found these.

(HOWARD enters.)

MERCER *(Into buzzer)* Hello? *(No answer.)* They must have the wrong door.

HOWARD It's kids. They do that to me all the time.

(A distant pounding on the downstairs door.)

MERCER Whoever it is wants in. *(The buzzer sounds again. THERESA goes to the window. Into buzzer)* What? *(No answer. Into buzzer)* Linda? *(No answer. The buzzer sounds again. Into buzzer)* Who is it? *(No answer. The pounding again.)*

THERESA *(Looking out the window)* Oh my God! *(She steps back.)* It's him!

HOWARD *(Going to the window)* Get away from the window!

MERCER *(Overlapping)* Where?

THERESA I saw him! It's him!

HOWARD *(Quickly, jumping back)* Oh Christ, that's the guy!

THERESA *(Overlapping)* Call the police. Call the police! *(She grabs at Howard's coat pocket for his phone. He extracts it and she grabs it.)*

HOWARD We should follow him!

MERCER I'll go. *(He grabs the pan from the box and runs out the door. THERESA dials 911.)*

HOWARD Be careful! *(Overlapping with her call. He closes the door and locks it, then moves between the window and* THERESA.*)* Stay away from the window.

THERESA *(Overlapping, on phone)* I want to report an . . . an intruder. I have a protective order, he's violating a protective order . . . 354 East 74th. Second floor . . . Theresa Bedell . . . I don't know! . . . Hurry! *(She hangs up and stands for a second.)* If they . . . if they . . . if they can catch him, if they catch him . . . *(Beat.)* If they catch him I won't have to leave.

HOWARD The sorry son of a bitch.

THERESA I won't have to leave.

HOWARD I know.

(Long pause.)

THERESA When I was in college, my parents were killed in a car wreck. My brother had already graduated. But he drank too much and he lost his job and he couldn't stop drinking. And I let him live with me once, but he stole from me and I had to ask him to leave. And I haven't heard from him in six years. I don't know where he is.

HOWARD It's okay.

THERESA I wanted you to know that about me.

(Pause. The buzzer sounds.)

HOWARD *(Into buzzer)* Yeah?

MERCER *(On speaker)* It's me. Let me up.

*(*HOWARD *buzzes him up.)*

THERESA *(Angry)* Why is he back?

HOWARD He saw me, I think. When I looked out the window.

THERESA He can't just get away!

HOWARD I should have snuck down the back. I could have caught him out front.

THERESA Maybe Mercer saw where he went, though. If the police get here . . .

HOWARD I know.

THERESA If the police get here in time . . .

HOWARD I know. Theresa. I know. It's okay.

THERESA No, it's not.

HOWARD I know. I'm sorry

(A knock on the door.)

MERCER *(From offstage)* It's me.

*(*HOWARD *lets him in.)*

HOWARD Did you see him?

MERCER *(Out of breath)* He disappeared. I don't know where he went.

THERESA But did you see him?

MERCER I never even saw him. There's . . . he could have gone anywhere.

(Beat.)

HOWARD What were you going to do with that?

MERCER What?

HOWARD The pan? Fry him an egg? *(*MERCER *puts the pan down. Beat. They are all on edge, but with no way to release it.)* This is no good. It's no good. *(*MERCER *goes to the window, looks out. Nothing. Pause.* HOWARD *looks around.)* Leave all this stuff. Theresa? Leave it.

THERESA I want my letters. *(She walks over to the shoebox* *and picks it up.)* I don't think he found my letters. *(She pulls out a card in a bright envelope.)* There's nothing in here. Some letters my mom wrote me one summer when I went to camp. *(She looks at the letters and starts to cry.)*

MERCER Hey. Hey. *(He goes to her.)* Why don't you look at those later?

(He gently takes the box from her. HOWARD fishes around in a pocket and pulls out a handkerchief and gives it to her.)

HOWARD It's fairly clean.

(THERESA blows her nose. Pause. HOWARD looks for some way to help her.)

MERCER What's the new name?

THERESA What?

MERCER You're changing your name tomorrow. What did you pick?

THERESA Claire.

HOWARD That's pretty.

MERCER Claire what?

THERESA Howells.

HOWARD Howells. Where have I heard that?

THERESA William Dean Howells.

MERCER Of course.

HOWARD Claire Howells. It's very nice.

(Beat.)

THERESA I don't want it.

HOWARD You don't like it?

THERESA I don't want it. I don't want to change my name. I don't want to go to Denver. I don't want to write sports. I don't like snow. *(HOWARD and MERCER don't know how to answer.)* I want my old name back.

HOWARD Claire is very pretty. *(Sounding it out)* Claire. *(Beat.)* Mercer, this is Claire.

MERCER *(Extends his hand.)* How do you do? *(THERESA doesn't take his hand.)* This is Howard.

HOWARD Very pleased. *(Beat.)* You know, I hear in Denver the hot tub comes included in every apartment.

MERCER Really? Well, I hear that they have a major league baseball team there. I believe they're called the Colorado Forty-niners.

THERESA Stop it. If you're nice . . . if you're nice, that makes it harder.

(Pause. They stand. Then THERESA holds out her hand to MERCER.)

MERCER You want your letters?

THERESA Yeah.

(MERCER gives them to her. Beat. THERESA holds out her hand again.)

MERCER What?

THERESA Claire Howells.

MERCER *(Shakes her hand.)* Mercer Stevens.

(THERESA holds out her hand to HOWARD. He shakes it.)

HOWARD Howard Siegel.

THERESA Claire Howells.

(HOWARD picks up the top of the shoebox and hands it to her.)

HOWARD You don't want those to spill. *(Suddenly she hugs him tightly, crying.)* Hey hey. *(For a moment they stand.)* Shhh. Shhh.

(They part, and she turns and hugs MERCER. *He hugs her back, then she steps back.)*

THERESA It's the Colorado Rockies.

MERCER I knew that.

THERESA Where are the cops?

HOWARD They're coming.

THERESA I don't like it in here. *(Small beat.)* I used to, though. I used to like it in here.

MERCER Maybe we could wait outside?

HOWARD I don't think we should.

(The buzzer sounds. MERCER *gets it.)*

MERCER Yeah?

POLICEWOMAN *(On buzzer)* You called the police?

MERCER *(In buzzer)* We'll be right down. *(To* THERESA*)* It should be okay now.

(They start to leave. HOWARD *waits to turn off the light.)*

THERESA No. Leave the light on.

HOWARD You think?

THERESA In case he's watching. I don't want him to know I've left.

(They exit, leaving the light on, closing the door behind them.)